EYEWITNESS TRAVEL TOP 10

SANTA FE, TAOS, & ALBUQUERQUE

NANCY MIKULA

Left **Santuario de Chimayó** Center **A Guadalupe Street scene** Right **Exhibit, Museum Hill**

LONDON, NEW YORK,
MELBOURNE, MUNICH AND DELHI
www.dk.com

Reproduced by Colourscan, Singapore
Printed and bound in China by South
China Printing Co. Ltd.

First American edition 2006
09 10 9 8 7 6 5 4 3 2 1
Published in the United States by
DK Publishing, 375 Hudson Street, New
York, New York 10014

Reprinted with revisions 2009

**Copyright 2006, 2009 ©
Dorling Kindersley Limited**

ISSN 1479-344X
ISBN: 978-0-7566-3253-3

Within each Top 10 list in this book, no
hierarchy of quality or popularity is
implied. All 10 are, in the editor's
opinion, of roughly equal merit.

Contents

Santa Fe, Taos, & Albuquerque's Top 10

The information in this DK Eyewitness Top 10 Travel Guide is checked regularly.
Every effort has been made to ensure that this book is as up-to-date as possible at the time of
going to press. Some details, however, such as telephone numbers, opening hours, prices,
gallery hanging arrangements, and travel information are liable to change. The publishers
cannot accept responsibility for any consequences arising from the use of this book, nor for
any material on third party websites, and cannot guarantee that any website address in this
book will be a suitable source of travel information. We value the views and suggestions of
our readers very highly. Please write to: Publisher, DK Eyewitness Travel Guides,
Dorling Kindersley, 80 Strand, London WC2R 0RL.

Cover: Front – **DK Images:** Tony Souter clb; **SuperStock:** age fotostock main. Spine – **DK Images:**
Francesca Yorke b. Back – **DK Images:** Tony Souter cl; Francesca Yorke c, cr.

Left **Crucifixes for sale, Albuquerque** Right **A house in Santa Fe**

Left **A street scene from Santa Fe** Right **New Mexico Museum of Natural History and Science**

Key to abbreviations
Adm *admission charge* **Dis. access** *disabled access*

SANTA FE, TAOS, & ALBUQUERQUE TOP 10

TOP10 Santa Fe, Taos, and Albuquerque Highlights

Contemporary, vibrant "City Different," Santa Fe is the nation's oldest capital city and a magnet for lovers of art, history, fine cuisine, and outdoor activities. Taos offers stunning mountain landscapes that draw numerous working artists, whose studios and galleries are some of the major attractions. Albuquerque, one of the region's fastest growing cities, is well known for its fascinating museums.

1 Old Town Santa Fe
World-renowned art galleries, museums, and restaurants, all housed in Santa Fe-style adobe buildings *(see pp8–9).*

20 ⌐——— miles ¬ 0 ⌐ km ——— ┐ 20

2 Canyon Road
This mile-long stretch of road up the canyon delivers an unforgettable mix of Southwest, traditional and contemporary art galleries, sculpture gardens, shops, and restaurants that attract art buyers and visitors from the world over *(see pp12–13).*

3 Georgia O'Keeffe Museum
The world's largest permanent collection of paintings by this celebrated New Mexican artist. Special exhibits of her work are often paired with paintings by her contemporaries *(see pp14–15).*

4 Museum Hill
Four exceptional museums present Native American art, history and culture, folk art from around the globe and Spanish Colonial artifacts. The museums are linked by paths and a central plaza with stunning mountain vistas *(see pp16–17).*

5 Guadalupe Street/ Historic Railyard District
Old warehouses converted into exciting artists' studios, restaurants, and shops provide an upbeat energy to Santa Fe *(see pp18–19).*

Map labels: Abiquiu Reservoir, Gallina, Regina, Coyote, Cuba, Jemez Mountains, Lagunitas, San Miguel, La Cueva, Tiniar, La Ventana, Jemez Springs, Torreon, Jemez Pueblo, Ponderosa, San Ysidro, Zia Pueblo, Puerco River, Algodones, Bernalillo, Rio Rancho, Alameda, Albuquerque Old Town, 8

Downtown Santa Fe

Taos Old Town

Working artists and visitors are drawn to the stunning natural beauty and free spirit of Taos. It has great galleries, restaurants, historic buildings, and museums *(see pp20–21)*.

Taos Pueblo

Continuously occupied by Pueblo Natives since 1400, these multistoried adobe buildings set against a backdrop of towering mountains are a United Nations World Heritage Site *(see pp22–23)*.

Albuquerque Old Town

Historic buildings and shops encircle a plaza, while nearby museums showcase New Mexico's artists and landscape *(see pp26–27)*.

El Rancho de las Golondrinas

Costumed interpreters and festivals bring the past alive at this hacienda complex, once the last stop before Santa Fe along the Camino Real route *(see pp28–29)*.

Bandelier National Monument

Home to the Ancestral Pueblo people, the towering rock cliffs of Pajarito plateau are filled with natural and hand-dug cave dwellings that stand above the remnants of the streamside village of Tyuonyi *(see pp30–31)*.

A good place to plan your trip is at the excellent website www.newmexico.org

🔟 Old Town Santa Fe

Missouri merchant William Becknell (see p35) opened the Santa Fe Trail in 1821, making Santa Fe the vibrant crossroads of two important trade routes. Its rich fusion of Native American, Mexican, and European influences is reflected in the unique adobe architecture. The varied heritage can also be seen in an array of galleries, museums, restaurants, and boutiques, as well as the historic shop-lined streets and plazas.

Sculpture, St. Francis Cathedral

Façade, Institute of American Indian Arts Museum

🍴 The Blue Corn Café & Brewery *(see p69),* located in Plaza Mercado, serves New Mexican food and pub fare.

🅿 Parking is cheap and available in the parking lot behind St. Francis Cathedral. Enter from Alameda.

• Map D4
• Sena Plaza: Entrance near 125 E Palace Ave; dis. access
• Burro Alley, between San Francisco St & Palace Ave

Top 10 Sights

1. The Plaza
2. St. Francis Cathedral
3. Palace of the Governors
4. San Miguel Mission Church
5. Sena Plaza
6. La Fonda
7. Museum of Fine Arts
8. Institute of American Indian Arts Museum
9. Burro Alley
10. Loretto Chapel

1 The Plaza

The Santa Fe Plaza *(above)* bustles with hordes of people, sitting under the trees, or shopping at a marketplace event. It marks the terminus of the Santa Fe Trail, the area where the trade wagons were unloaded in the 1800s.

2 St. Francis Cathedral

This Romanesque cathedral *(above)* was designed in France for Santa Fe's first archbishop, Jean Baptiste Lamy. *La Conquistadora,* the oldest Madonna statue in the US, resides in the northeast side chapel *(see p65).*

3 Palace of the Governors

This is the oldest public building in the US. It was built in 1610 as Spain's seat of government in the area. Today, it is the Museum of New Mexico *(left)* and the best place to learn about local history *(see p63).*

During summer, early morning is the best time to enjoy the Plaza without too many people.

4 San Miguel Mission Church

The country's oldest church still in use, San Miguel Mission Church *(right)* dates from the earliest days of Santa Fe. Great art objects abound, including the 800-lb (363-kg) San Jose Bell, cast in Spain in the 14th century *(see p37)*.

5 Sena Plaza

Originally the hub of the Sena mansion, this serene garden courtyard is surrounded by colorful shops. The entrance to Sena Plaza is through one of the small doorways from the street.

6 La Fonda

Known as the "Inn at the End of the Trail", this hotel was used by traders and politicians from the opening of the Santa Fe Trail in 1821. The current inn *(right)* was built in 1922, and the artistic interior means it is still popular *(see p64)*.

7 Museum of Fine Arts

This 1917 adobe building became the model for the Santa Fe architectural style. It displays works by the Taos Society of Artists and the Santa Fe Society of Artists *(see p41)*.

8 Institute of American Indian Arts Museum

The museum has raised Native American art to its world-class stature. Native artist Allan Houser provided direction in the early days. The changing exhibits show works of artists, faculty, and students *(see p43)*.

9 Burro Alley

Burros carried firewood on their backs *(right)* down this notorious alley lined with gambling halls in the 1830s and 40s. Today, it houses the celebrated French café, Café Paris Bakery.

10 Loretto Chapel

The choir loft of this lovely Gothic church has a "Miraculous Staircase" which makes two full 360 degree turns without a central support *(below)*. An unknown carpenter built the circular wooden staircase *(see p64)*.

Oldest Capital City

La Villa de Santa Fe, the oldest capital city in the US, was founded in 1610 as New Mexico's capital and Spain's administrative center for the area. At 7,000 ft (2,133 m) in the valley between the Jemez and Sangre de Cristo mountain ranges, Santa Fe was the trade route link between the historic Camino Real route from Mexico and the Santa Fe Trail to Missouri in the 1800s. Taverns lined the streets of old Santa Fe, and the bustling Plaza was the scene of many gunfights.

New Mexico is the only state with "USA" on its license plates.

Left **Portrait Gallery** Center **Traditional jewelry** Right **Governor L. B. Prince Reception Room**

TOP 10 Palace of the Governors

1 The Building
The 1610 adobe building has been modified over the years. The defense towers have been removed, and the porch along the front was added in 1913. In the Governor's Room, it is possible to see how one of the adobe walls was constructed.

2 Native Portal
Since the late 1800s, Native American artists have been selling handmade jewelry under the portal. Vendors change daily, and the permission to sell there is obtained by lottery.

3 Lew Wallace Room
Governor Lew Wallace wrote the famous classic, *Ben Hur*, here. The room houses the Segesser Hide Paintings, the first to show Spanish colonial life in America and illustrate a 1720s expedition ambushed by Native Americans

Bust of Lew Wallace, Lew Wallace Room

4 Mexican Governor's Office
This room is a re-creation of the Mexican governor's office circa 1845, with a corner beehive fireplace and period furnishings, such as the handwoven rug on the floor and the painted chest.

5 Portrait Gallery
Portraits of local luminaries, like Don Diego de Vargas, Jean-Baptiste Lamy, General Stephen W. Kearney *(see p35)*, and Padre Martinez are displayed here.

6 New Mexico Chapel
The chapel is a reconstruction created from early photographs and furnished with religious art objects from 1821 to 1880. The result is an excellent depiction of 18th-century chapels found throughout New Mexico.

7 Governor L. Bradford Prince Reception Room
This is an exact replica of the room as it appeared for a Legislative reception on February 13, 1893. Great attention has been taken to match details in a photograph taken that day.

8 Art of Ancient America
Ancient American artifacts include ceramic effigies of animals, fruits, and people. This permanent exhibit has Middle American and Andean pottery, and art objects prior to European contact, from 1500 BC to AD 1500.

9 Changing Exhibit Rooms
A major changing exhibit examines different aspects of New Mexico history. One of the recent shows explored the role of Jewish immigrants during the late 19th and early 20th centuries.

10 Palace Press
The historically authentic Museum of New Mexico's 19th-century print shop produces limited edition books, pamphlets, and cards on antique print presses.

The free docent-led tours, conducted throughout the day, provide a historical overview of the area. Call 505-476-5100 for times.

Top 10 Historical Artifacts on Exhibit

1 Segesser Hide Paintings (1720–50)
2 Bland Mud Wagon, Santa Fe Trail (1800s)
3 State Seal (1912)
4 Pancho Villa Clock (1916)
5 Tiffany silver service set (1918)
6 19th-century traveling desk
7 Handcrafted rawhide violin
8 16th-century Morion Helmet
9 Westward Ho pressed glass (1876)
10 Rio Grande blankets

History of the Palace of the Governors

Built in 1610 by Don Pedro de Peralta (see p35) and the settlers of early Santa Fe, this adobe building was the government house for Spain when Popé, a San Juan priest, led the Pueblo Revolt of 1680 (see p34). The building continued to be controlled by Pueblo Natives until the Spanish returned in 1693 led by Don Diego de Vargas. Mexico declared independence from Spain in 1821, and Mexican rule began under Facundo Melgares. American General Stephen Kearney arrived from Missouri along the Santa Fe Trail in 1846 after the United States declared war on Mexico. Before long, Mexican Governor Manuel Armijo and many citizens of Santa Fe fled, and Santa Fe became the seat of government for the new United States Territory under Governor Charles Bent (see p36). During the American Civil War, Confederate soldiers used the Palace as temporary headquarters in 1862. A year before New Mexico became the 47th state, in the early 1900s, the Palace of the Governors opened as the first site of the Museum of New Mexico. Free docent tours are available daily. Contact the museum directly for tour schedules: 505-476-5100.

Bland Mud Wagon used on the Santa Fe Trail

A view of the Native Portal, busy with visitors

TOP 10 Canyon Road

Signage outside a local gallery

A vibrant art scene, predominantly contemporary and historic Southwestern, draws art buyers and visitors from around the world to Canyon Road. The street often takes on a festive air as people stroll its length, visiting the galleries, enjoying sculpture gardens and flower-filled spaces. Much of the art is high quality and priced to match, though some galleries offer affordable works for the new collector. Wearable art is featured in a few of the clothes and jewelry boutiques.

Local art on sale on Canyon Road

🍵 At the top of Canyon Rd, The Teahouse *(see p68)* serves over 100 varieties of tea.

East of Canyon Rd, Downtown Subscription *(see p68)* café offers coffee and snacks, as well as some major dailies and magazines.

🕐 Friday evenings the galleries stay open late and hold street performances and special art shows.

• Map L5
• Nathalie: 505-982-1021; partial dis. access
• El Zaguán and Gardens: 505-983-2567
• Wiford Gallery and Sculpture Garden: 505-982-2403
• Geronimo Restaurant: 505-982-1500; dis. access
• Randall Davy House and Audubon Center: 505-983-4609; open 9am–5pm daily

Top 10 Sights

1. Nathalie
2. Morning Star Gallery
3. Hudson Gallery and Seven-O-Seven Contemporary
4. El Zaguán and Gardens
5. Zaplin Lampert Gallery
6. Photo Eye Gallery
7. Wiford Gallery and Sculpture Garden
8. Geronimo Restaurant
9. Cristo Rey Church
10. Randall Davy House and Audubon Center

1 Nathalie
Designer boutique featuring fashionable Southwestern-style clothes and accessories. The designs are original and the style reflects the owners' European tastes.

2 Morning Star Gallery
The superb gallery has a collection of museum-quality Native American art, including rare examples of pottery, rugs, sculptures, and textiles *(see p66)*.

Galleries at Canyon Road

3 Hudson Gallery and Seven-O-Seven Contemporary
A unique international collection of traditional paintings and sculpture, as well as modern and contemporary art is housed in this gallery *(see p39)*.

4 El Zaguán and Gardens
Off Canyon Road, this garden *(left)* is an ideal pause from gallery shopping. Open to visitors, the Spanish Pueblo-style late 19th-century hacienda with a row of bricks at the roof line, is occupied by the Historic Santa Fe Foundation.

Acequia Madre parallels Canyon Road, and makes a lovely return route along a pretty residential street.

7 Wiford Gallery and Sculpture Garden
One of the best contemporary art galleries and a truly fascinating sculpture garden.

10 Randall Davy House and Audubon Center
Located at the top of Upper Canyon Road, the 135-acre Audubon Center is an architectural gem, with lovely walking trails into Santa Fe Canyon. Artist Randall Davy's former home *(below)*, a remodeled 1847 saw mill, is open for tours Monday afternoons.

5 Zaplin Lampert Gallery
This gallery features works by the early artists of Taos, Santa Fe, and the American West, such as A. Bierstadt and Edward S. Curtis *(see p38)*.

6 Photo Eye Gallery
Just off Canyon Road on Garcia Street, this gallery showcases the work of contemporary photographers.

8 Geronimo Restaurant
Housed in a beautifully preserved 1700s adobe, the famed restaurant has a Territorial-style portal.

9 Cristo Rey Church
The church *(below)* marked the 400th year of Spanish entry. The 150,000 adobe blocks used to build it were made by the parishioners *(see p45)*.

The Art and Soul of Santa Fe
Canyon Road began as a Native American trading trail along the Santa Fe River. The Spaniards used it to bring firewood from the mountains into Santa Fe to sell in Burro Alley *(see p9)*. Later, small adobe houses and farms were built along the road. In 1920, a group of young artists, "Los Cinco Pintores", built homes just off the road to "bring art to the people". Today, some 80 galleries along "The Art and Soul of Santa Fe" attract visitors with their wealth of traditional and contemporary fine art.

The best way to get to the Randall Davy House and Audubon Center is to drive – be aware that the last section of the road is dirt.

13

TOP 10 Georgia O'Keeffe Museum

New Mexico's most popular art museum is dedicated to the dramatic art of Georgia O'Keeffe (1887–1986). It houses the largest permanent collection of over 1,100 works from her early years in Texas and New York, through her time in Abiquiu and Ghost Ranch (see p95). The small, stylish museum displays only a fraction of her works at any time.

Façade of Georgia O'Keeffe Museum

Interior of Georgia O'Keeffe Museum

🎨 The museum displays at least 50 of O'Keeffe's works at all times, but none of the paintings has a fixed position. It closes several times each year to change exhibits. Call 505-946-1000 for schedule.

🍷 For a glass of wine and a sit-down Southwestern meal, try the O'Keeffe Café next door (505-946-1065).

For a quick lunch or snack, head over to Zélé Café *(see p68).*

• Map H3
• 217 Johnson St
• Open Jun–Oct 10am–5pm daily, 5pm–8pm every Fri; Nov–May closed Wed
• Adm $8, $7 for seniors, $4 for students & New Mexico residents; free 5pm–8pm Fri
• Docent tours 10:30am daily
• www.okeeffemuseum.org

Top 10 Features

1. Early Abstracts
2. Progressive Series
3. Adobe and Abiquiu
4. Skulls and Flowers
5. Animal Bones
6. Flowers and Plants
7. Close-Up Flowers
8. New Mexico Landscapes
9. Landscapes from Above
10. Urban Landscapes

1 Early Abstracts
O'Keeffe was a highly individualistic artist. Intrigued by the wide skies and dramatic scenery of Texas, she created abstract depictions of nature and landscape, including themes as intangible as the sounds and emotions of storms.

2 Progressive Series
O'Keeffe *(below)* often created an entire series on a single subject, progressing from a representative view to an abstract image. Her last major flower series depicts the progress of a flower, from a flower head to an enormous single pistil.

3 Adobe and Abiquiu
The adobe home O'Keeffe bought in Abiquiu enthralled her. The door into the patio, in particular, became the subject of numerous paintings, such as *Black Patio Door* and *Patio with Cloud.* Adobe buildings appeared in many of her paintings – she frequently depicted portions of softly contoured walls or doors.

Don't miss the O'Keeffe sculpture in a small courtyard that is accessed from inside the museum.

Skulls and Flowers
4 While walking through New Mexico desert country, O'Keeffe was intrigued by the complex, hard forms of animal skulls and soft, colorful flowers, and they became two of her favorite subjects. To her, they represented complementary natural forces, and she often juxtaposed them in her works *(above)*.

Animal Bones
5 The desert near Taos, with its sun-bleached animal bones, captivated O'Keeffe. Over the years she painted bones in non-traditional ways, capturing the blue sky and clouds through pelvic holes.

Flowers and Plants
6 Some of O'Keeffe's best-known works are her flowers *(center)*. Focusing on a single blossom, she often created many views of the flower on different canvases, twisting and turning the perspective to capture the curves, contours, and textures that fascinated her.

Close-Up Flowers
7 Bold and provocative in color, shape, and form, O'Keeffe's flower canvases *(above)* were often seen as being representative of female anatomy. The artist, however, insisted that her flowers were neither female nor sexual.

New Mexico Landscapes
8 The Southwestern landscape dazzled O'Keeffe. Many of her landscapes depict the mountains and river valleys in the region.

Landscapes from Above
9 In the 1950s, O'Keeffe began traveling by airplane, which gave her work a new perspective as she depicted the land from above. These paintings show ribbon-like rivers curving through landscapes and mountain valleys. All of the boundaries are soft and without definition.

Urban Landscapes
10 Following the uproar over her allegedly erotic flower close-ups, O'Keeffe concentrated for a while on semi-abstractions of clearly identified objects. She was living at the time in a New York City skyscraper, and painted city buildings from her window *(above)*.

Museum Guide

Call ahead for hours and exhibit information, as the gallery closes between exhibitions several times each year. The audio tour, available when you purchase admission tickets, is a good way to learn more about individual pieces in the collection, as well as about Georgia O'Keeffe and her artistic progression. Don't miss the 12-minute film in the museum theater.

TOP 10 Museum Hill

This distinctive complex of four exceptional museums offers a rich diversity of experiences. You will find here the history of the Native American world of arts and culture, a stunning array of clever toys, Spanish Colonial art objects, as well as unique collections of Native American jewelry. Milner Plaza offers sculptures, fountains, a great café, and wonderful views of the Sangre de Cristo Mountains.

The Museum of Indian Arts and Culture

An exhibit at the Museum of International Folk Art

🍴 **Museum Hill Café** at Milner Plaza serves light meals (505-820-1776) 11am–3pm Tue–Sun.

ℹ️ **Here, Now and Always**, Buchsbaum Gallery, and Changing Native American Exhibits constitute the Museum of Indian Arts and Culture *(see p81)*. The Museum of International Folk Art includes the Girard Wing, Neutrogena Wing, and Hispanic Heritage Wing *(see p81)*.

Drive to Museum Hill or take the "M" bus from Santa Fe Plaza (505-955-2001).

• Map L3
• On Camino Lejo off Old Santa Fe Trail
• Wheelwright Museum of the American Indian: 704 Camino Lejo; 505-982-4636; open 10am–5pm Mon–Sat, 1–5pm Sun; donation; dis. access; www.wheelwright.org

Top 10 Sights

1. Buchsbaum Gallery of Southwestern Pottery
2. Here, Now and Always
3. Changing Native American Exhibits
4. Milner Plaza
5. The Museum of Spanish Colonial Art
6. Journey's End
7. Wheelwright Museum of the American Indian
8. Hispanic Heritage Wing
9. Neutrogena Wing
10. Girard Wing

1 Buchsbaum Gallery of Southwestern Pottery

Exceptional ceramics from the Pueblos of New Mexico and Arizona show the development of pottery from the earliest days to the present, including changing displays from contemporary potters.

2 Here, Now and Always

This exhibit at the Museum of Indian Arts and Culture tells the story of the Pueblo, Apache, and Navajo peoples through their artworks *(below)* and their words, incorporating multimedia and special effects.

3 Changing Native American Exhibits

Several shows present contemporary and traditional art. A recent exhibition covered prehistoric trade with Mexico.

4 Milner Plaza

This central Plaza *(above)* offers views of the mountains, as well as sculptures, a labyrinth and easy access to the two largest museums. Several markers show the original path of the Santa Fe Trail.

Each museum offers a handout and free docent tours with admission, and has restrooms and a gift shop.

⁵The Museum of Spanish Colonial Art

The exhibits *(right)* at this John Gaw Meem-designed adobe home trace the evolution of art traditions, from Spain to Latin America and New Mexico *(see p81).*

⁹Neutrogena Wing

Exhibits *(center)* from around the world feature here. Multimedia displays heighten the festive theme. A recent exhibit, Dream On, featured beds from Europe and Asia.

¹⁰Girard Wing

A dazzling collection of folk art includes objects from across the world. The highlights are ceramic figures *(above)* arranged in various cultural scenes, including a Mexican and a Peruvian village.

⁶Journey's End

Bronze sculpture, by Reynaldo Rivera and Richard Borkovetz, captures the travails faced along the Santa Fe Trail. The scene shows a mule skinner and lead caravan wagon approach Santa Fe, watched by a Pueblo woman, a boy, and a dog.

⁷Wheelwright Museum of the American Indian

This 8-sided, Navajo *hogan*-type building displays changing exhibits of contemporary and traditional Indian art. The Case Trading Post is the gift shop and is a replica of an early trading post.

⁸Hispanic Heritage Wing

The country's finest selection of Spanish Colonial and Hispanic folk art is housed here *(left)*. Familia Fe (Family and Faith) presents religious artifacts as well as practical objects used by the early Spanish settlers in New Mexico.

Gallery Guide

The main entrance to the complex is from the parking lot below Milner Plaza. At the top of the stairs, the Visitors' Center is on the right, and the Museum Hill Café is to the left. From the center of the Plaza, the Museum of Indian Arts and Culture is to the left. Downhill and beyond the Museum of Indian Arts is the Museum of Spanish Colonial Art. To the right of the Plaza is the Museum of International Folk Art. Downhill and beyond is the Wheelwright Museum of the American Indian.

The courtyard of the Wheelwright Museum of the American Indian displays sculpture by renowned Native American artists.

🔟 Guadalupe Street/Historic Railyard District

Lined with beautifully remodeled adobe homes and warehouses converted to house studios and shops, Guadalupe Street presents an upbeat Santa Fe experience. It is also the departure point for scenic rail trips on the Santa Fe Southern Railway. A comprehensive development will bring a new park and theater, as well as studio space for emerging artists.

A colorful mural on Guadalupe Street

🍴 **For a snack or a full meal, stop at Zia Diner** *(see p50)*. **It is located at 326 S Guadalupe St.**

- Map G2
- SITE Santa Fe: 1606 Paseo de Peralta; 505-989-1199; open 10am–5pm Wed, Thu, & Sat, 10am–7pm Fri, 12 noon–5pm Sun; adm $8, students & seniors $4, free on Fri (free docent tours with adm); dis. access
- Farmers' Market: Cerrillos Rd & Guadalupe St; 505-983-4098; open mid-Apr–mid-Nov Tue & Sat mornings; partial dis. access
- Sanbusco Market Center: 500 Montezuma; 505-989-9390; open daily, schedules vary by shop; dis. access
- Santa Fe Southern Railway: 410 S Guadalupe St; 505-989-8600; open daily, call for schedules; adm to depot free; partial dis. access
- New Mexico Film Museum: 418 Montezuma Ave; 505-476-1860
- Evo Gallery: 554 S Guadalupe St; 505-982-4610

Top 10 Sights

1. Santuario de Guadalupe
2. SITE Santa Fe
3. Farmers' Market
4. Evo Gallery
5. Sanbusco Market Center
6. Design Center
7. Converted Warehouses
8. Santa Fe Southern Railway
9. Murals
10. New Mexico Film Museum

1 Santuario de Guadalupe

This small sanctuary *(above)* is the oldest shrine in the United States to Mexico's patron saint, Our Lady of Guadalupe. The exceptionally beautiful Baroque altar screen shows the Virgin of Guadalupe and the Holy Trinity created by José de Alzibar in 1783 *(see p45)*.

2 SITE Santa Fe

This non-profit organization showcases emerging international and local artists. A variety of programs, including concerts and gallery shows, are available.

3 Farmers' Market

One of the best farmers' markets *(left)* in the country features more than 75 booths. Organic foods include fresh-picked locally grown produce, including meats, cheeses, and chiles. Flowers and crafts are also available. The market has a festive air and the vendors are friendly and enjoy talking about their food and crafts. Saturday mornings have more booths than Tuesdays.

Changes occur frequently in this vibrant, fast-growing area so check www.sfrailyardcc.org for the latest information.

4 Evo Gallery

Contemporary and cutting-edge abstract works predominate at this gallery (left), which features a variety of shows by established and emerging artists.

5 Sanbusco Market Center

Specialty stores for fly fishing and pets, upscale clothing boutiques, and many exciting restaurants are found here (left).

6 Design Center

The eclectic center of galleries and studios displays exhibits (below) in various artistic styles: contemporary, tribal, African, and pop-Surrealism.

7 Converted Warehouses

Among these are New Mexico's largest Ceramic Art Center, Santa Fe Clay, and Warehouse 21, a teen center for arts.

Historic Railyard District

A spur line was built from Lamy for the Atchison, Topeka & Santa Fe Railroad and the first train arrived in 1880. In 1887, the Denver & Rio Grande Railroad extended their narrow-gauge tracks to Santa Fe. Later still, the New Mexico Central Railroad ran a line southward to connect the El Paso & Rock Island Railway Line. The only track still in use is the old AT&SF line to Lamy, acquired by the Santa Fe Southern Railway in 1992.

8 Santa Fe Southern Railway

Railcars (above) travel through the high desert to either the rim of the Galisteo Basin for panoramic views, or to the town of Lamy.

9 Murals

Colorful murals (below) adorn several buildings on Guadalupe Street, breaking the neutral colors of Santa Fe adobe, and enhancing the area's artistic flavor.

10 New Mexico Film Museum

Currently being built, this museum will highlight the state's film industry and will incorporate the Jean Cocteau Theatre.

From April to October, Santa Fe Southern Railway organizes a Friday evening sunset trip with cash bar, and a Saturday barbecue trip.

Taos Old Town

Less commercial than ultra-chic Santa Fe, this classic old Western town blends Hispanic, Native American, and Western Anglo cultures. Its desert landscape has attracted a steady stream of working artists since the 1920s. The streets, where heroes of the Wild West once strode, are now lined with galleries and shops.

Local favorite, Bent Street Café & Deli

🍴 For a good breakfast, lunch, and dinner in all price categories try Bent Street Café & Deli *(see p93)*.

🛍 Many of the best shops and galleries are on Bent St, Kit Carson Rd, Paseo del Pueblo Norte, and Ledoux St.

- Map E2
- Hotel La Fonda de Taos: 108 South Plaza; 575-758-2211; dis. access; D.H. Lawrence Art adm $3; free for hotel guests
- Bert Phillips House: 136 Paseo del Pueblo Norte
- El Rincon Trading Post: 114 Kit Carson Rd; 575-758-9188

Top 10 Sights

1. Taos Plaza
2. Taos Art Museum at the Fechin House
3. Kit Carson Home and Museum
4. Long John Dunn House and Shops
5. El Rincon Trading Post
6. Hotel La Fonda de Taos
7. Governor Bent Home and Museum
8. The Harwood Museum of Art
9. Bert Phillips House
10. E.L. Blumenschein Home and Museum

Taos Plaza
Locals and visitors flock to the heart and social hub of Taos. Special events include Taos Plaza Live!, a popular Thursday evening summer concert series.

Taos Art Museum at the Fechin House
Renowned woodcarver and artist, Russian-born Nicolai Fechin moved to Taos in 1927. He added exquisite details to his adobe house (above), which today shows works by the Taos Society of Artists *(see p89)*.

Kit Carson Home and Museum
In 2005, the house *(above)* built by legendary guide, trapper, and agent, Kit Carson *(see p35)*, was extensively renovated, and transformed into a living history museum *(see p91)*.

A street in Taos Old Town

Long John Dunn House and Shops
Notorious entrepreneur and veteran gambler Long John Dunn's former home houses several lovely shops and restaurants arranged around a garden courtyard *(below)*.

Taos Plaza Live! is held every Thursday 6 to 8pm, from June to mid-September. For more information call 575-758-8800.

5 El Rincon Trading Post

In 1909, Ralph and Rowena Meyers opened the first trading post to preserve vintage artifacts. Today it has a museum and gift shop *(left)*.

6 Hotel La Fonda de Taos

The classic Pueblo Revival-style building *(right)* offers shops and fine dining, as well as the D.H. Lawrence paintings that were seized by the London police in 1929 for being too risqué.

7 Governor Bent House and Museum

New Mexico's first governor was scalped and killed here in 1847 by an angry mob protesting against American rule. Today, the museum *(below)* displays period objects and some of his personal household possessions *(see p36)*.

Taos Society of Artists

Artist Joseph Sharp *(see p39)* visited Taos in 1893 to produce illustrations of Taos Pueblo. He returned East, proclaiming the area's artistic grandeur. In 1898, artist Bert Phillips settled in Taos, and began promoting it as an artistic mecca. Before long, other artists began arriving from the East. In 1915, these artists, along with Ernest Blumenschein, Oscar Berninghaus, E. Irving Couse, and Herbert Dunton founded the Taos Society of Artists.

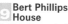

8 The Harwood Museum of Art

Dedicated to Taos artist Burt Harwood, the museum houses the works of the Taos Society of Artists *(see p90)*.

9 Bert Phillips House

Built in the early 1800s, the home of artist Bert Phillips *(see p39)*, which he remodeled in 1905, is a significant landmark, even though it is not open to the public.

10 E.L. Blumenschein Home and Museum

The museum displays the family possessions *(above)* and art collection of this artist, as well as works by other Taos artists *(see p91)*.

Taos Pueblo

Never conquered, the Pueblo people still live on their traditional tribal lands in Taos Pueblo's famous North and South Houses, believed to have been built during AD 1000–1450. These strikingly beautiful ancient adobe buildings stand in a valley beneath the towering peaks of the Sangre de Cristo Mountains. A crystal clear mountain stream runs through the pueblo, and still provides drinking water for the 100 or so residents of the sacred village. There is no electricity and no running water in this UNESCO World Heritage Site.

Top 10 Sights

1. North House/Hlaauma
2. South House/Hlaukkwima
3. San Geronimo Church
4. The Red Willow Creek
5. Horno
6. Drying Rack
7. Ladders
8. Pueblo Shops
9. Defensive Wall
10. Cemetery and Site of Old Church Ruins

Taos Pueblo depicted on an old postcard

○ Native-run food stands are ideal for Native foods such as bread baked in outdoor ovens.

Michael's Kitchen serves snacks and full meals from 7am–8:30pm daily (304 Paseo del Pueblo Norte Rd).

○ Native-run shops inside the pueblo usually open about 10am.

• Map E2
• Located at the north end of Taos Pueblo Rd
• 575-758-1028
• www.taospueblo.com
• Open winter: 8am–4pm daily; summer: until 4.30pm daily; closed late winter to early spring
• Adm $10 adults, $5 students, children free, camera fee $5 for personal use only
• Partial dis. access

1 North House/Hlaauma

This strikingly handsome multistoried adobe building *(center)* stands beneath sacred Taos Mountain. Little has changed since Spanish explorers first saw it in 1540, except the doors and windows that were added later.

2 South House/Hlaukkwima

Like North House, South House is over 1,000 years old and built entirely of adobe. *Vigas (see p67)* create the roof structure, with *latillas* (small sticks) placed crosswise.

4 The Red Willow Creek

The only source of drinking water, the creek *(left)* carries water from Taos Mountain into the village. It also divides the village into north and south, with foot bridges connecting them.

3 San Geronimo Church

The 1850 church *(right)* is one of the newest buildings here. The Virgin Mary is the central figure, brought by the early Spanish missionaries. Many Pueblos blend Catholic practices and ancestral rituals.

Horno

5 These outdoor, domed adobe ovens *(above)* are used primarily to bake bread, pastries and other goods. Spanish in origin, the ovens, or *hornos* as they are known in Spanish, came into use after Spanish settlers arrived in Taos valley.

Drying Rack

6 The racks *(below)* were used to cure animal hides for clothing, as well as for preserving Native foods. Meat was dried to create jerky, while wild berries and harvested corn were dried before storing them for winter.

Ladders

7 Originally, there were no doors or windows in the buildings. Residents had to climb ladders to the rooftop and then descend through a hole in the roof. The ladders could be pulled up when enemies approached.

Pueblo Shops

8 Many of the first-floor homes open as shops to sell an array of local arts and crafts, including sculpture, paintings, and pottery. Vendors also sell traditional foods.

Defensive Wall

9 The wall surrounding the pueblo was originally used to protect and defend the village against enemies. It was once 10-ft (3-m) tall with several lookout towers.

Cemetery and Site of Old Church Ruins

10 The original 1619 San Geronimo Church was rebuilt in 1706. In 1847, it was burned in retaliation to Pueblo participation in the massacre of Governor Bent *(see p36)*. Only the original bell tower remains, and the area is a holy cemetery *(right)*.

Pueblo Guide

Drive north on Paseo del Pueblo Norte (NM 68) for two miles past the Taos post office and watch for signs on the right directing you to the pueblo. Visitors must comply with rules of etiquette *(see p112)*. They were established to protect the privacy of the residents and to preserve the village and the Pueblo culture. Some areas of the village are restricted, do not enter them.

Left **Straw mats on display at Here, Now and Always** Right **Colorful Native American textile**

🔟 Native American Culture

1 Museum of Indian Arts and Culture

The museum's major wing, Here, Now and Always, provides a fine introduction to Native American history, art, and culture *(see p81)*.

2 Indian Pueblo Cultural Center

Owned by the 17 Pueblo tribes, this museum presents their culture and customs, as well as the history of this area, from the Pueblo people's perspective. Native American dances and artistic events are presented on summer weekends *(see p98)*.

3 Pow Wow

The Albuquerque Gathering of Nations Pow Wow and Taos Pueblo Pow Wow *(see p58)* host Native American dances. The Grand Entrance draws elaborately costumed dancers from tribes across North America. Contests are held, and booths offer traditional items.

4 Taos Pueblo

This UNESCO World Heritage Site is one of the most visited places in New Mexico. The adobe buildings here have been continuously inhabited by Native Americans for over 1,000 years *(see pp22–3)*.

5 Palace of Governors Portal

This is one of the best places to buy Native American art as it is strictly controlled for quality. It also provides a chance to interact with Native American artists, who enjoy discussing their art *(see p10)*.

6 Indian Market

Every August, 1,200 Native American artists gather in Santa Fe Plaza for an entire weekend to sell their art. This is an excellent place to learn about and shop for Native American jewelry and art and sample traditional cooking at the food booths *(see p58)*.

7 Bandelier National Monument

One of the best places to learn about ancestral Pueblo history. Start at the Visitor's Center to view the exhibits and see the short film, *The Bandelier Story*. Walk the trail to the Long House, and view the ruins of Tyuonyi, the ancient Pueblo settlement *(see pp30–31)*.

8 Petroglyph National Monument

This National Monument, surrounding five extinct volcanoes, has more than 20,000 petroglyph images that were cut into the rocks centuries ago by Native American hunting parties as they traveled through the area *(see p97)*.

9 San Ildefonso Pueblo

Best known as the home of Maria Martinez and her internationally famous black-on-black pottery, this pueblo has a thriving arts community that

Guided tours are sometimes available for a fee, and in summer are often led by helpful Pueblo college students.

welcomes visitors. Many artists sell their work from their homes or the trading post. ◈ *Map D4*
* *23 miles (37 km) N of Santa Fe*
* *505-455-3549 • Open 8am–5pm daily, museum 8am–4pm weekdays*
* *Adm $5 per vehicle, non-commercial camera permit $10–20*

Mission Church, by taking an hour-long guided tour. ◈ *Map A6 • Off Hwy I-40 • 505-552-7860 • Open early Apr–late Oct 8am–5pm daily, tours 8am–5pm; late Oct–early Apr 8am–6pm daily, tours 8am–3pm • Adm $10, non-commercial camera permit $10 • Partial dis. access • www.skycity.com*

Acoma Pueblo

10 Known as "Sky City", the pueblo sits dramatically atop a 367-ft (112-m) high mesa chosen for defense. Visitors can explore one of the oldest continuously occupied villages in the US, and the lovely San Esteban del Rey

A panoramic view of the Acoma Pueblo

Pueblo Feast Days

One of the most interesting times to visit a pueblo is on Feast Days, when you can watch Native American ceremonial dancing and enjoy the festivities. Each pueblo has a feast day nominally honoring the Catholic saint for whom the village was named by the Spanish. However, the festivities are based on ancient seasonal ceremonial rituals that control the pace and rhythm of the event. Festivities usually take place in the plaza, with lines of costumed dancers moving to drums while chanting. Food booths are often available after the religious events. It is recommended to call ahead to verify date, time, location, and to ask any questions you may have about the ceremony. Photography restrictions are often more stringent than usual, and it is considered impolite to ask questions about a ceremony while it is in process (see p112).

Left **Pueblo people playing painted drums** Right **Dancers celebrating Pueblo Feast Day**

Albuquerque Old Town

Some of the Southwest's greatest museums, historic buildings, and the Plaza with the lovely San Felipe de Neri Church are the highlights of Old Town. Fiesta time brings the Plaza alive with mariachi bands and brightly costumed dancers. Don't miss the dinosaur exhibits at the Museum of Natural History and Science, the famed paintings by the Taos Society of Artists at Albuquerque Museum of Art and History, the funky Rattlesnake Museum, and the eclectic Turquoise Museum.

Historic Route 66 sign

An exhibit at the American International Rattlesnake Museum

🍽 For excellent New Mexican food, eat at the Church Street Café *(see p101)*, in one of the oldest houses in the city (2111 Church St).

- Map C6
- Old Town Visitors' Center: 303 Romero St NW; open daily 9am–4:30pm
- National Atomic Museum: 1905 Mountain Rd NW; 505-245-2137; www.atomicmuseum.com; open daily 9am–5pm; adm $5, $4 seniors and children

Top 10 Sights

1. Albuquerque Plaza
2. San Felipe de Neri Church
3. New Mexico Museum of Natural History and Science
4. Albuquerque Museum of Art and History
5. Turquoise Museum
6. Route 66 and Central Avenue
7. National Atomic Museum
8. Albuquerque Aquarium and Rio Grande Botanic Gardens
9. American International Rattlesnake Museum
10. Explora!

Albuquerque Plaza

Dating from 1706, the Plaza is a serene place to relax, with plenty of grassy areas and benches. Shops, restaurants, galleries, and historical buildings surround the Plaza.

New Mexico Museum of Natural History and Science

The world's longest dinosaur *(above)*, a simulated volcano, and Ice Age cave are some of the exhibits at this interactive museum. Superb visual and audio effects *(see p97)*.

San Felipe de Neri Church

The twin spires and Gothic details of this lovely church *(above)* were added during 1861–90. The small museum displays 17th-century artifacts *(see p97)*.

Albuquerque Museum of Art and History

One of the finest collections of Southwestern art, including outstanding works by the Taos Society of Artists, and other regional artists *(see p97)*.

If you are planning to visit the Albuquerque Museum of Art and History, park in the free lot there, and explore Old Town afterwards.

5 Turquoise Museum

This family-run museum highlights turquoise *(left)*, the most popular gem used in the jewelry of the Southwest. Visitors can explore the displays and learn about the many varieties of turquoise, as well as how it is mined *(see p99)*.

6 Route 66 and Central Avenue

Part of historic Route 66, Central Avenue forms the southern boundary of Old Town, retaining many of its old buildings.

7 National Atomic Museum

The museum *(below)* is devoted to the history of nuclear weapons and atomic energy. The central focus is on the bomb. The artifacts include replicas of the famous first two atomic bombs, "Little Boy" and "Fat Man".

8 Albuquerque Aquarium and Rio Grande Botanic Gardens

The aquarium offers a variety of intriguing marine life *(below)*. The Botanic Gardens have walled gardens and glass conservatories *(see p98)*.

9 American International Rattlesnake Museum

Home to the largest collection of live rattlesnakes in the world. Rattlers from North, Central, and South America are displayed in glass tanks that simulate their habitats *(see p43)*.

10 Explora!

The interactive exhibits at this children's museum *(below)* inspire creative exploration of science and art. Children can ride the high-wire bicycle, or create a soap bubble with themselves inside *(see p56)*.

Albuquerque and the Missing "R"

Old Town was started by Provincial Governor Don Francisco Cuervo y Valdés. He obtained a land grant from Spain in 1706, despite not having the required 30 families. Cleverly, he named the proposed town after the viceroy of New Spain, the Duke of Alburquerque. The Duke was pleased, and issued the land grant. It was much later, in the early 1800s that the first "r" was gradually dropped from the spelling, and from then on the city has been known as Albuquerque.

La Glorieta at 1801, Sandia Theatre at 1816, and Tower Court at 2210 are some of the original buildings on Central Avenue/Route 66.

🔟 El Rancho de las Golondrinas

For travelers along El Camino Real, the most vital trade route from Mexico, this historic Spanish Colonial ranch was the last stopping place, or paraje, before arriving in Santa Fe. Caravans of traders, soldiers, and other travelers paused at "the Ranch of the Swallows" to rest and to graze their livestock in the grassy meadows along the river. These adventurers not only brought books, medicine, tools, and fabric from around the world, but also their beliefs and know-how, as well as the news of the day. Today, costumed interpreters bring the past alive.

Detail in the courtyard, El Rancho de las Golondrinas

🍴 Food is available during festival and event weekends.

🚗 From Santa Fe, take exit 276 and bear right on NM 599. Turn left at the traffic light onto Frontage Rd. Turn right just before the race track on Los Pinos Rd.

• Map D5
• 334 Los Pinos Rd, 15 miles (24 km) S of Santa Fe, off Interstate 25
• 505-471-2261
• Open Jun–Sep 10am–4pm Wed–Sun
• Adm $5 adults, $4 seniors & teens, $2 children
• Dis. access
• Guided tours: Apr–Oct; 505-473-4169; adm $45 for group, plus individual fee
• Civil War (May); Festival weekends: Spring Festival (Jun), Wine Festival (Jul), Summer Festival (Aug), Harvest Festival (Oct); call for hours & adm

Top 10 Sights

1. Golondrinas Placita Courtyard
2. Kitchen
3. Chapel
4. Raton Schoolhouse
5. Weaving Workroom
6. Grandmother's House
7. Big Mill from Sapello
8. House of Manuel Baca
9. Mora House
10. Country Store

1 Golondrinas Placita Courtyard
The earliest buildings were built in a defensive square. The central *placita* was a place for meeting, grinding corn, drawing water from the well, and baking.

2 Kitchen
Here, the shepherd's wife hung herbs and chiles *(below)* from the ceiling to dry, kept her baby in a swinging crib, and cooked in clay pots. The shepherd's bed was over the corner cooking fireplace.

3 Chapel
The chapel, with painted wooden *reredos (below)*, is located in a main room of the original ranch. The 14 Stations of the Cross are on the side walls.

4 Raton Schoolhouse
Spanish children studied in their homes, or in Mexican boarding schools until the late 1800s. This 1880 building, the first school in Raton, was rebuilt here in 1980.

5 Weaving Workroom
Handmade looms were used in fine weavings, which were a popular barter item. Skilled weavers, mostly men, made their own natural dyes, and created lovely patterns.

The Visitors' Center offers a free, short film to introduce the ranch.

6 Grandmother's House

In the late 1800s, a grandmother would sometimes live apart from the family in a very simple cottage *(above)*. Here, she would help with family chores and care for the younger children, teaching them old traditions as well as domestic skills, ensuring that these were passed on from one generation to the next.

7 Big Mill from Sapello

The mill *(below)* was made in New York and shipped to New Mexico by railroad in the 1880s. It was used to make flour for the soldiers at Fort Union until the fort closed in 1891.

Festivals and Events

For about 12 weekends, during June to early October, festivals and theme weekends are held at El Rancho de las Golondrinas. Additional costumed interpreters are there to operate the mills and take part in the daily farm and domestic activities of the place. Entertainers enhance the festive feel as they perform the old music, dances, and plays, while craftsmen demonstrate and sell their traditional wares. Food is also available for purchase.

8 House of Manuel Baca

Three rooms remain from the larger house, which was built in the 1830s, once a defensive *placita* was no longer needed.

9 Mora House

This town house is a fine example of the Spanish architecture found in the late 1800s when milled lumber became available.

10 Country Store

The small store *(left)* sold items produced on the ranch to travelers using El Camino Real. Religious objects, blankets, candles, tobacco, cloth, and grain were available.

On festival days, a costumed miller operates the water-powered Big Mill from Sapello to grind flour.

🔟 Bandelier National Monument

Set in the rugged cliffs and canyons of Pajarito Plateau, Bandelier National Monument shelters the remains of an ancestral Pueblo settlement. From the 12th to 16th century, successive communities settled here, hunting and growing corn and squash. The earliest occupants carved out cave dwellings from the volcanic rock of the towering cliffs, while later people built houses from talus (rock that has fallen from the cliffs). The Main Loop Trail leads past Tyuonyi to cave homes and the Long House, multistoried homes built into the cliff.

A panoramic view of the cliff

🍴 Limited menu snack bar is available next to the Visitors' Center.

The closest eateries are in Los Alamos.

🎬 Stop in the Visitors' Center to watch the orientation film, *The Bandelier Story*.

Mornings and late afternoons are the best times to visit in the summer, as the desert trail through the monument offers limited shade and the midday sun is very hot.

• Map C4
• Located on NM 4, 48 miles (77 km) NW of Santa Fe
• 505-672-3861
• www.nps.gov/band
• Open daily, closed Dec 25 & Jan 1
• Visitors' Center: Open Memorial Day to Labor Day 8am–6pm, fall & spring 9am–5:30pm
• Adm $10 per vehicle (for a week)
• Dis. access

Top 10 Sights

1. Cave Kiva
2. Big Kiva
3. Small Kiva
4. Tyuonyi
5. Cave Rooms
6. Canyon Panorama
7. Petroglyphs
8. Pictograph and Bat Cave
9. Long House
10. Talus House

Cave Kiva
Men would have done the weaving in this sacred kiva. The reconstructed sticks on the ceiling were used for loom supports, while the floor depressions served as anchors.

Big Kiva
Primarily meant for religious ceremonies, it is thought that this underground structure *(above)* was probably also used as a place to educate boys and young men into the village traditions.

A kiva meant for ceremonies

Small Kiva
These three ceremonial kivas are the size usually found in the Southwest. The first of them has been excavated and stabilized.

Tyuonyi
The village of Tyuonyi *(left)* was at least two stories high, with about 400 rooms that would have housed about 100 people.

Plan to arrive in the morning when it is less busy, especially in late spring and summer when the monument is most visited.

Cave Rooms
These cave rooms *(left)* were dug out of the south-facing soft cliff walls. The walls were plastered with clay, and the ceilings still have soot from the fires that were used for light, heat, and cooking.

Canyon Panorama
Frijoles Canyon contains a permanent stream in desert country where water is scarce, facilitating the growth of crops and sustaining animals used for food. Around 500 people once lived in the canyon.

Long House
The Long House community extended 800 ft (240 m) along the cliff wall. The early inhabitants lived in these adjoining multistoried stone homes that often had another hand-carved cave room in the back.

Talus House
The cliff was once lined with many houses built of *talus*. These were often three or four stories high, all supported by the canyon wall *(below)*.

Petroglyphs
Above the top row of round *viga* holes *(see p67)*, are many petroglyphs, which are line drawings carved into the stone *(above)*. The carvings are believed to represent people, birds, and animals.

Pictograph and Bat Cave
The pictograph, or painted design, was found on the back wall of a second-story dwelling. A colony of bats sometimes occupies the cave *(left)* above the pictograph.

Monument Guide
The best place to begin is at the Visitors' Center in Frijoles Canyon. Friendly staff can assist with trip planning. Museum displays and an orientation film are helpful, and there are trail guides available for the self-guided walks through the monument. Plan to walk the paved Main Loop Trail that starts near the Visitors' Center in about an hour. The monument covers a vast area, and there are 70 miles (113 km) of trails to hike if you want to see additional ruins.

The highest cave is accessible only by climbing 140 ft (42.7 m) on four ladders.

Left **Rio Grande Valley** Center **"Fat Man"** Right **The Santa Fe Trail**

10 Moments in History

1 Rise of the Pueblos

The ancestors of modern Pueblo peoples first arrived in about AD 600. Continued droughts forced more Native Americans from the Southwest to relocate to the drought-resistant Rio Grande Valley in AD 1000. Further drought intensified the migrations. The adobe pueblos were built around this time, including Acoma and Taos Pueblos (see pp22–3).

2 First Spanish Expedition (1540–42)

In a quest for the fabled Seven Cities of Gold, Francisco Vásquez de Coronado led 300 Spanish conquistadores and 1,000 Native Americans in the first European expedition into the Southwest. He probably wintered near Santa Fe, at Kuaua Pueblo.

3 Spanish Settlement (1598)

In 1595, Juan de Oñate was commissioned by King Philip II of Spain to found a settlement in New Mexico and convert the Native Americans to Christianity. More than 200 men, some with families, several Franciscan friars, and thousands of livestock traveled the El Camino Real, reaching San Juan in July 1598, where the first settlement was established.

A lithographic portrayal of Juan De Oñate (1595)

4 Santa Fe Capital of New Mexico (1610)

Founded in 1607, La Villa de Santa Fe, "The City of Holy Faith," became capital of New Mexico in 1610 under the leadership of Pedro de Peralta. Construction of the Palace of the Governors (see p63) began in 1610, using adobe and Pueblo-style architecture.

5 Pueblo Revolt (1680)

After 80 years of Spanish rule, the Pueblos united for the first time under Popé, an able warrior from San Juan Pueblo. After a violent battle, the Spanish surrendered and 2,500 settlers retreated to El Paso. The only successful Native American uprising in the US, the Pueblo Revolt drove the Spanish from Santa Fe for 12 years.

6 Santa Fe Recaptured for Spain (1692)

Led by soldier and negotiator Governor Diego de Vargas, the re-conquest of New Mexico lasted two years. The fateful event is celebrated in a popular annual festival (see p58). In 1693, Spanish settlers returned to Santa Fe only to meet armed resistance from the Pueblo people. Many died on both sides before hostilities ended in 1694.

Preceding pages: **Bandelier National Monument**

Bustling wagon train on the Santa Fe Trail

Mexico Gains Independence (1821)

7

A newly independent Mexico welcomed open trade with the US. Loaded wagon trains poured down the Santa Fe Trail, which was the first major trade route into the Southwest. Subsequently, Santa Fe became the trading hub for the region.

New Mexico Becomes a US Territory (1846)

8

After the US declared war on Mexico, General Stephen Watts Kearney and his forces entered Santa Fe on August 18, 1846.

New Mexico Becomes a State (1912)

9

By 1912, when New Mexico became a state, it had been discovered by the artists. Santa Fe was already discussing adoption of a Pueblo Revival architecture. In 1915, the Taos Society of Artists was formed.

Manhattan Project (1942–45)

10

This secret government project, headed by J. Robert Oppenheimer and others, took over a boys' school at Los Alamos to develop the first atomic bombs: "Little Boy" and "Fat Man." The site was chosen for its remoteness, and the project went from theoretical concept to a working bomb in just 36 months. Los Alamos is still home to the world's most advanced nuclear facilities.

Top 10 Santa Fe Figures

1 **Francisco Vásquez de Coronado (1510–54)**
Coronado led the first European exploration into New Mexico.

2 **Juan de Oñate (1550–1626)**
Founder of the first Spanish settlement, Oñate extended El Camino Real into New Mexico.

3 **Don Pedro de Peralta (1584–1666)**
Spanish-born governor of New Mexico established Santa Fe as the capital city of New Mexico.

4 **Don Diego de Vargas (1643–1704)**
Spanish governor led the re-conquest of Santa Fe and New Mexico after the Pueblo Revolt.

5 **William Becknell (1788–1865)**
He opened the Santa Fe Trail in 1821, and led the first wagon train into the town in 1822.

6 **Dona Tules (1804–52)**
Close to Governor Armijo and General Kearney, Tules ran a gambling house and bordello.

7 **General Stephen Watts Kearney (1794–1848)**
Kearney was Commander of the Army of the West during the War with Mexico.

8 **Archbishop Jean Baptiste Lamy (1814–88)**
Santa Fe's first Bishop was behind the construction of St. Francis Cathedral *(see p65)*.

9 **Kit Carson (1809–68)**
Legendary Southwestern guide and Native American spy, he was as national hero.

10 **J. Robert Oppenheimer (1904–67)**
Theoretical physicist and director of the Manhattan Project, he led the creation of the first atomic bombs.

Mexican-born Dona Tules's actual name was Gertrudis Barceló.

Left **Zuni Pueblo dancers at Bandelier National Monument** Right **Taos Pueblo**

🔟 Historic Sites

1 Palace of the Governors
During the Pueblo Revolt of 1680, Native Americans laid siege to Santa Fe. The Spanish captured the palace, killing scores of Native Americans during the battle. When the latter diverted the palace water supply, the Spanish surrendered and agreed to leave the tribal lands and head to El Paso *(see p63)*.

2 Taos Pueblo
Built between AD 1000 and 1450, the pueblo suffered an attack following the murder of Governor Bent in 1847. In 1970, Taos Pueblo won back from the US government 48,000 acres, including their sacred Blue Lake high in the Sangre de Cristo Mountains *(see pp22–3)*.

3 Bandelier National Monument
Although numerous archeological sites have been identified here, less than 50 have been excavated. The most accessible is Frijoles Canyon, where a well traveled trail leads to unique cliff dwellings *(see pp30–31)*.

4 Governor Bent House and Museum
After the US war with Mexico, many people welcomed US rule. However, pockets of resistance remained. Following New Mexico's annexation, Charles Bent of Taos was appointed the first governor. In 1847, he was killed in his home by Spanish and Indians loyal to Mexico. The murder of Bent set off a violent reprisal against Taos Pueblo.
◈ *Map P2* • *117 Bent St, Taos*
• *575-758-2376* • *10am–5pm daily* • *Adm*

5 Los Alamos
In 1939, Albert Einstein wrote a letter to President Franklin D. Roosevelt suggesting that a new type of powerful bomb might be the outcome of a nuclear chain reaction. In 1943, in the midst of World War II, the small town of Los Alamos became the top-secret location for the Manhattan Project *(see p35)*, which built the atomic bombs dropped on Japan in August 1945. ◈ *Map C4*
• *Information Center, 109 Central Park Sq*
• *505-662-8105*

6 Petroglyph National Monument
The world's largest accessible collection of petroglyphs is carved into the black rocks of this

Indian petroglyphs on a basalt boulder

➲ *In the reprisal following Governor Bent's murder, 150 people died in Taos Pueblo when the church they sought refuge in was burned.*

forbidding volcanic landscape. Most of the more than 15,000 ancient petroglyphs were carved by the ancestors of today's Native Americans from AD 1300 to 1650. Early Spanish settlers contributed more carvings as well. Several trails lead past large numbers of petroglyphs (see p97).

Church of San Francisco de Asis

7 San Miguel Mission Church

Constructed in the early 17th century by Tlaxcalan Indians, who were Spanish servants, this simple adobe structure is one of the oldest churches still in use in the US. During the Pueblo Revolt of 1680, the church was one of the first buildings to fall. ◈ Map K5 • 401 Old Santa Fe Trail • 505-983-3974 • Open 9am–5 pm Mon–Sat, 9am–4pm Sun • Adm

8 St. Francis Cathedral

The present cathedral was built in 1886 on the site of Santa Fe's first church, destroyed during the Pueblo Revolt of 1680. When New Mexico became a US Territory in 1846, Jean Baptiste Lamy, the first archbishop, had the cathedral designed by French architect Antoine Mouly (see p65).

Sculpture, St. Francis Cathedral

9 Church of San Francisco de Asis

In 1814, the founding families of Rancho de Taos built this simple, yet gracefully elegant adobe Mission church. They could never have dreamt that the softly rounded curves, double bell towers, and buttresses would come to inspire artists around the world. It was a favorite subject of Georgia O'Keeffe (see p73).

10 Coronado State Monument

The monument is named for Francisco Vásquez de Coronado (see p35), who arrived in this valley in 1540 with 300 soldiers and 1,000 Native Central American allies from New Spain on the first Spanish expedition into this area. Kuaua Pueblo, first settled around 1300, was located here till about the late 16th century. Probably, Coronado headquartered at the pueblo. The Kuaua Pueblo ruins and Pre-Columbian murals found here are worth seeing (see p82).

Above **A contemporary work displayed at Hudson Gallery**

Art Galleries

1 Gerald Peters Gallery

This gallery is well known for its quality 19th- and 20th-century Classic Western works, and 20th-century modern and contemporary American art. There's also a sculpture-filled courtyard and a fine-art bookstore (see p66).

2 Morning Star Gallery

Native American art and artifacts are displayed in this gallery, specializing in historic and contemporary textiles, pottery, and sculpture. An intriguing selection of works is also on offer for new collectors (see p66).

3 Zaplin Lampert Gallery

The gallery houses works by 19th- and early-20th century Western artists, including Albert Bierstadt and George Catlin. Also here are works of early Western photographer Edward S. Curtis and a select group of early Modernists and contemporary painters and sculptors.
⊗ Map L2 • 651 Canyon Rd • 505-982-6100 • Dis. access

4 Nedra Matteucci Galleries

The gallery presents top works by early Taos and Santa Fe artists, besides rare examples of American Impressionism and Modernism, Russian Realism, and contemporary art. The pretty outdoor sculpture garden exhibits prized pieces (see p66).

An exhibit, Morning Star Gallery

5 Altermann Galleries

This nationally recognized gallery specializes in American Western Art from the 19th century to current times. The collections include original works by painter, sculptor, and illustrator Frederick Remington, as well as landscape artist Thomas Moran. The outdoor sculpture garden presents monumental bronze sculptures, and the gallery conducts four auctions annually. ⊗ Map L5 • 225 Canyon Rd • 505-983-1590 • Dis. access

6 Shidoni Foundry, Galleries, and Sculpture Garden

A captivating display of large figurative and abstract sculpture fills a spacious park-like meadow. Inside, galleries display sculpture, furniture, glass, ceramics, and paintings by some of Santa Fe's finest working artists (see p76).

Shidoni's Sculpture Garden

Bronze pouring occurs most Saturdays in Shidoni Foundry, and is open to the public.

A painting by Leigh Gusterson, The Taos Gallery

7 The Taos Gallery
This stylish gallery features the work of contemporary artists from around the Southwest. Themes celebrating nature and the natural world are rendered in sculptures, high-quality, limited edition prints, oils, and water-colors, as well as jewelry and fine art photography (see p92).

8 Total Arts Gallery, Inc
Drawing on the talents of a worldwide, eclectic assortment of contemporary artists, the owners of this Taos gallery present a delightful collection of painting and sculpture (see p92).

9 Hudson Gallery and Seven-O-Seven Contemporary
This chic pair of galleries present a collection drawn from a renowned group of international artists. Hudson Gallery focuses on more traditional paintings and sculpture, while Seven-O-Seven offers a divergent collection, often in unusual media. **◈** Map L2 • 707 Canyon Rd • 505-820-1888

10 Mission Gallery
One of New Mexico's oldest galleries. In the former home of Taos artist Joseph Henry Sharp, it shows works by early Taos artists and the "New Mexico Moderns," who were painters who merged abstraction with Native American themes in the 1900s (see p92).

Top 10 Artists and Influencers

1 Joseph Henry Sharp (1859–1953)
Painter of North American culture and founding member of the Taos Society of Artists.

2 Bert G. Phillips (1868–1956)
Founding member of the Taos Society of Artists, known for his renderings of Taos Indians.

3 Ernest Blumenschein (1874–1960)
Prominent American painter, and founding member of the Taos Society of Artists.

4 John Gaw Meem (1894–1983)
Renowned architect and an important advocate of Pueblo Revival-style architecture.

5 Patrociño Barela (1908–64)
Self-taught master artist and woodcarver, he developed the Barela Style.

6 Mabel Dodge Luhan (1879–1962)
New York socialite, responsible for attracting Georgia O'Keeffe and D. H. Lawrence to Taos.

7 Georgia O'Keeffe (1887–1986)
Celebrated artist, best known for her flower close-ups and New Mexican landscapes.

8 Maria Martinez (1887–1980)
Created distinctive black-on-black finish pottery (see p24) at San Ildefonso Pueblo.

9 R. C. Gorman (1932–2005)
Prolific artist known for his depiction of Navajo women going about their daily life.

10 Allan Houser (1915–94)
Internationally-acclaimed sculptor and painter.

Allan Houser also served as an instructor at the Institute of American Indian Arts Museum see p43.

Left **Folk art mural** Center **Museum of Indian Arts and Culture** Right **A Navajo blanket**

☝10 Major Museums

1 Georgia O'Keeffe Museum

New Mexico's most famous resident artist loved the high desert sun and the clarity of form it brought to her favorite flowers and landscapes. This museum has the largest collection of her paintings *(see pp14–15)*.

2 Museum of International Folk Art

This unique museum presents a dazzling collection of folk art from around the world. Some of the best works are found in the Girard Wing, which showcases colorful toys, tools, textiles, and everyday items. Dioramas filled with ornate, hand-carved figures depict subjects such as Heaven and Hell, South American villages, or an Indian street scene. A painting of St. George and the Dragon occupies a wall near a ceramic drum from Morocco and opera figures from China *(see p81)*.

Display, Museum of International Folk Art

3 Museum of Indian Arts and Culture

From prehistoric petroglyphs to cutting-edge contemporary Native art, this outstanding museum presents the cultural and artistic story of the Indians of the Southwest. Collection highlights include Mimbres and Anasazi ceramics, and early black-on-black pottery by Maria Martinez, as well as modern works such as the mythically surreal images of David Bradley *(see p81)*.

4 New Mexico Museum of Natural History and Science

With world-class dinosaur displays, including the world's longest dinosaur, this museum presents the natural history of New Mexico through interactive exhibits. Experience an erupting volcano, explore a stalactite-filled cave, learn about the sea coast, or manipulate a full scale model of the Mars explorer. The LodeStar planetarium has shows several times a day *(see p97)*.

5 Museum of Art and History

With a fine collection of paintings by the Taos Society of Artists, this museum is also known for its works by members of Santa Fe's Cinco Pintores and the Transcendental Painting Group. The historical exhibit of Spanish arms and armor is impressive, as are the displays on 400 years of Albuquerque history *(see p97)*.

Inside The Museum of Spanish Colonial Art

Virgin at the Palace of the Governors

Pueblo dancer, Indian Pueblo Cultural Center

Anderson-Abruzzo International Balloon Museum

Located next to the Fiesta Park where the annual Balloon Festival occurs, Albuquerque's newest museum features soaring gallery spaces that contain the world's most extensive collection of modern and historic balloons and their memorabilia. Named for two of the city's legendary balloonists, the exhibits relate the use of balloons in adventure, warfare, and space exploration, and include artifacts that date from the earliest days of ballooning *(see p98).*

Palace of the Governors

The Museum of New Mexico since the early 1900s, this 1610 building has served as the seat of government under Spanish, Mexican, and American rule. In 2008, the current collections will be moved to a new museum Annex. The palace will be restored and furnished to portray the different periods of Santa Fe's history *(see p63).*

Museum of Fine Arts

The changing exhibits represent the region's best-known artists, who made Santa Fe one of the world's premier art centers. The St. Francis Auditorium hosts chamber music concerts and lectures. ✆ *Map J3 • 107 W Palace Ave, Santa Fe • 505-476-5072 • Open 10am–5pm Tue–Sun; 5pm–8pm Fri • Adm*

The Museum of Spanish Colonial Art

The Pueblo Revival-style building is adorned with tin light fixtures and hand-carved ceiling beams. The exhibits include a fascinating range of Rio Grande textiles, straw appliqué designs, decorative tin and ironwork, pine furniture, and other finely executed everyday objects used by early settlers. Many religious artworks are also on display including ornate carvings *(see p81).*

Indian Pueblo Cultural Center

The displays at this Pueblo-run museum, while a bit dated, offer intriguing insights into the culture, beliefs, and history of each of the 19 pueblos. The weekend courtyard events present live dancing, baking, and craft demonstrations *(see p98).*

Left **Fechin House** Center **An exhibit, Millicent Rogers Museum** Right **Ghost Ranch**

Specialty Museums

1 Los Alamos Historical Museum

The museum displays artifacts from the "Secret City" that created the world's first atomic bomb. The art center's large log building is a National Historic Landmark.
⊗ Map C4 • Central & 20th St, Los Alamos• 505-662-4493 • Open 10am–4pm Mon–Sat, 1pm–4pm Sun

2 Taos Art Museum at the Fechin House

The works of the early Taos Society of Artists and Taos Moderns are displayed in an adobe home. Famed artist Nicolai Fechin remodeled the house, filling it with woodcarving and furniture. Prominent exhibits include the works of Fechin, Bert Phillips, Joseph Sharp, and E.L. Blumenschein *(see p89)*.

Herbert Dunton's *Ginger*, Harwood Museum

3 The Harwood Museum of Art

The must-see exhibit is the octagonal gallery featuring seven large paintings by internationally acclaimed artist Agnes Martin. The Hispanic Traditions gallery presents the largest museum-owned collection of sculptures by 20th-century artist Patrociño Barela, as well as religious carvings donated by Mabel Dodge Luhan. There are works by the Taos Society of Artists and Taos Moderns as well *(see p90)*.

4 Bradbury Science Museum

The fascinating museum features interactive exhibits related to atomic weapons, nuclear energy, and technology. The development of the atomic bomb is well presented. The newest exhibits highlight the political and scientific challenges of maintaining the reliability of existing nuclear weapons in peacetime *(see p73)*.

5 Albuquerque Turquoise Museum

The family-owned museum boasts an exceptional collection of raw and refined turquoise stones and jewelry from more than 60 mines around the world. Displays show how turquoise differs from mine to mine. Visitors can learn about buying turquoise jewelry, as well as synthetic and "enhanced" stones that are common in today's jewelry markets *(see p99)*.

Millicent Rogers Museum

6 The outstanding museum houses more than 5,000 beautiful works of Native and Hispanic art. Displays include one of the largest collections of pottery by famed Native American potter Maria Martinez. Permanent and temporary exhibits showcase exceptional jewelry, handwoven textiles and baskets, paintings, pottery, *santos*, and Spanish Colonial furniture *(see p90)*.

Museums at Ghost Ranch

7 These two small museums display ceramics and fossils found during excavations in the area. The Florence Hawley Ellis Museum of Anthropology has ancient artifacts from the Paleo-Indian culture, while the Ruth Hall Museum of Paleontology shows fossils, including the tiny dinosaur, Coelophysis *(see p95)*.

Tinkertown Museum

8 This inspirational museum was constructed over a span of 40 years. Ross Ward (1941–2002) captured the essence of circus and small town life with miniature hand-carved wood figures. He traveled the world and collected memorabilia and antique toys to adorn the wonderfully intricate "villages" *(see p82)*.

Institute of American Indian Arts Museum

9 The superb museum collects and exhibits a wide range of 20th-century Native American arts. The institute and its artists have played a powerful role in the growth of contemporary Native American art. The innovative works by painters T.C. Cannon, Kevin Red Star, and Earl Biss introduced new trends in modern Native art in the 1960s.

Sculpture, Institute of American Indian Arts Museum

⌖ Map K4 • 108 Cathedral Pl, Santa Fe • 505-983-8900 • Open 10am–5pm Mon–Sat, 12–5pm Sun • Adm • www.iaiamuseum.org

American International Rattlesnake Museum

10 Dedicated to conservation and education, this compelling little museum has the world's largest collection of live rattlesnakes from North, Central, and South America. An introductory film explains the ecological importance of these often-misunderstood reptiles.

⌖ Map P5 • 202 San Felipe Dr N, Albuquerque • 505-242-6569 • Open 10am–6pm, 1pm–5pm Sun, closed pub hols • Adm

Left **St. Francis Cathedral** Center **Church of San Francisco de Asis** Right **Staircase, Loretto Chapel**

🔟 Cathedrals, Chapels, and Churches

1 St. Francis Cathedral

The French Romanesque-style structure offers a refreshing departure from the sea of traditional adobe buildings surrounding it. Designed in France and small by European standards, the St. Francis Cathedral was, nonetheless, a monumental undertaking for the Wild West town of Santa Fe in 1869. The project was directed by Santa Fe's first archbishop, Jean Baptiste Lamy, who passed away before the cathedral was completed in 1886. He is buried beneath the altar *(see p65)*.

2 Loretto Chapel

This charming chapel was commissioned by Archbishop Lamy, and was modeled after Sainte Chapelle in Paris. When completed in 1878, the building did not have a staircase to the choir loft, nor was there room to build a conventional staircase. Legend has it that the nuns of Loretto prayed for a solution, and an unknown carpenter with incredible skill appeared on the ninth day and built the "Miraculous Staircase" *(see p64)*.

Detail of intricately carved crucifix

3 Santuario de Chimayó

Known as the "Lourdes of America", this private chapel was built in the 1800s, following a vision by the landowner. Today, it is a pilgrimage site where thousands of worshipers arrive for a taste of the holy soil, which is believed to possess curative powers. Many notes, photos, and letters are displayed, attesting to the healing results of the earth *(see p75)*.

4 Church of San Francisco de Asis

One of New Mexico's most visited mission churches, San Francisco de Asis attracts parishioners, historians, and artists alike. It was built between 1710 and 1755, and in its early days, the church offered protection from attack as well as spiritual sanctuary. In the 1900s, Ansel Adams, Georgia O'Keeffe, and other

Colorful interior of Church of San Francisco de Asis

artists photographed and painted the lovely adobe church into art history *(see p73)*.

5 San Miguel Mission Church
Badly damaged in the Pueblo Revolt, the original adobe church was rebuilt and enlarged in 1710. Inside, the historic religious paintings and statues are impressive *(see p37)*.

6 Santuario de Guadalupe
Built between 1776 and 1795 by Franciscan missionaries, this chapel is the oldest shrine honoring Our Lady of Guadalupe, the patron saint of Mexico. It has a beautiful Baroque altar shrine. ⊛ *Map G4 • 100 S Guadalupe St, Santa Fe • 505-988-2027 • Open summer: 9am–12 noon, 1pm–4pm Mon–Sat; winter: Mon–Fri • Dis. access*

7 Cristo Rey Church
Designed by John Gaw Meem, proponent of Santa Fe's Pueblo Revival architectural style, this 1940 church is one of the world's largest 20th-century adobe buildings. ⊛ *Map M2 • corner of Canyon Rd and Cristo Rey, Santa Fe • 505-983-8528 • Dis. access*

8 San Felipe de Neri Church
The original church, started in 1706 by a Franciscan priest, was initially named San Francisco Xavier. However, the Duke of Alburquerque ordered that the titular saint be changed to San Felipe de Neri in honor of King Philip of Spain. The current church was constructed in 1793, when the first church collapsed *(see p97)*.

9 Holy Cross Catholic Church
Housing an exceptional collection of Spanish Colonial religious artifacts, this 1733

Inside elegant Holy Cross Catholic Church

adobe church offered sanctuary during a revolt against Mexican rule in 1837 and again during a rebellion against the US government in 1847 *(see p78)*.

10 San José de Gracia Church
Twin belfries with crosses, an exterior choir loft, and hand-painted *vigas (see p67)* and corbels adorn this 1760 adobe church. It is one of the finest examples of early Spanish Colonial church architecture in the Southwest. ⊛ *Map E3 • Las Trampas • Open Jun–Aug 9am–5pm Mon–Sat*

Left **Beautifully patterned rugs** Center **Religious images** Right **Cowboy hats for sale**

🔟 Shopping Areas

1 Old Town Santa Fe
The diverse boutiques and shops in Old Town range from chic to casually bohemian. Nicholas Potter (211 E Palace Ave) is Santa Fe's oldest bookstore, while Seret & Sons *(see p66)* stock exotica from around the world. The shops at La Fonda *(see p64)* present a wide range of clothing and art.

2 Canyon Road
This mile-long stretch of fabulous world-class art galleries has given Santa Fe its well-earned reputation as the predominant art-buying destination in America. A Friday night art walk adds the spectacle of street musicians to the gallery stroll *(see pp12–13)*.

3 Guadalupe Street/Historic Railyard District
Choose from an eclectic mix of antique and consignment shops, or swish one-of-a-kind boutiques. Check out the railroad souvenirs at the Santa Fe Southern Railway, or see the vintage quilts and antiques at Recollections *(see pp18–19)*.

4 Cerrillos Road
Best known for big-box stores, and strip malls. The Baca Street arts district has shops such as Celtic Jewelry and fanciful Liquid Light Glass. Nearby, Second Street offers refreshment breaks at the popular Cloud Cliff Bakery *(see p85)*.
🌐 *Map L2*

5 Bent Street
This charming street is known for its adobe shops and gardens. Parks Gallery and Brazos Fine Art offer Southwest contemporary art, while traditional art and Native Navajo blankets can be found at Robert Parsons Fine Art. Don't miss the cheerful John Dunn Shops and Bent Street Café & Deli.
🌐 *Map K2*

6 Kit Carson Road and Paseo del Pueblo Norte
The shops here are concentrated around the intersection of Kit Carson Road and Paseo del Pueblo Norte. Art from across the country is displayed at Nichols Taos Fine Art Gallery, while horses and New Mexican landscapes adorn the walls of the Farnsworth Gallery (1129 Paseo del Pueblo Norte). 🌐 *Map P2*

7 Rancho de Taos
The rancho's small collection of shops, galleries, and restaurants offers good shopping options. Chimayó Trading Del Norte (1 Ranchos Church Plaza) specializes in Navajo weavings, Pueblo and

Lavish interior of Seret & Sons in Old Town Santa Fe

Horse Feathers on 109-B Kit Carson Road (505-758-7457) has cowboy antiques and vintage Western wear.

Parks Gallery in Bent Street, Taos

Casa Grande pottery. Mesa's Edge (St. Francis Plaza) showcases fine gold and silver jewelry by regional artists. ✪ *Map E2*

Taos Plaza

Colorful shops around the Plaza are filled with regional arts, crafts, and souvenirs. Several fine galleries offer exceptional Native art. Visit Zane Wheeler Gallery (107-A Taos Plaza) for bright fabric art, and for contemporary landscapes and adobe scenes, try Grimshaw Fine Art (132 Kit Carson Rd). ✪ *Map P2*

Albuquerque Old Town

La Casita de Kaleidoscopes (326-D San Felipe) has one-of-a-kind and vintage kaleidoscopes, while Discover Balloons offers a large variety of balloon-festooned gifts and collectibles. Numerous art galleries offer Native American pottery, jewelry, and paintings. At Amapola Gallery (106 Romero St), 35 award-winning New Mexico artists display their work. ✪ *Map C6*

Nob Hill in Albuquerque

This original stretch of Route 66 and Central Avenue *(see p27)* is known for its trendy shops. Luxurious lingerie and jewelry are found at Martha's Body Bueno boutique (3105 Central Ave). Try Mariposa Gallery *(see p100)* for unique craft items. ✪ *Map C6*

Top 10 Unique Shops

1 Jackalope
Sun-bleached animal skulls, bright kitsch. ✪ *Map L2* • *2820 Cerrillos Rd* • *505-471-8539*

2 Buffalo Exchange
Vintage prom gowns, Western shirts, and designer jeans. ✪ *Map P6* • *3005 Central Ave NE* • *505-262-0098*

3 Double Take at the Ranch
Stocks vintage Western wear. ✪ *Map G4* • *321 S Guadalupe St* • *505-820-7775*

4 Travel Bug
Travel planning haven with a huge choice of travel books and maps. ✪ *Map L4* • *839 Paseo de Peralta, Santa Fe* • *505-992-0418*

5 ChocolateSmith
Delicious handcrafted chocolates. ✪ *Map L2* • *1807 2nd St, Santa Fe* • *505-473-2111*

6 Discover Balloons
Hot air ballooning giftshop. ✪ *Map P5* • *205-B San Felipe, Albuquerque* • *505-842-1111*

7 Chuck Jones Studio Gallery
Original artworks and prints by "Bugs Bunny" animator. ✪ *Map J4* • *135 W Palace Ave, Santa Fe* • *505-983-5999*

8 Moby Dickens Bookshop
Award-winning store, offers Native American and Western literature. ✪ *Map P2* • *124 Bent St, Taos* • *575-758-3050*

9 Maison Faurie
An expansive range of antiques, including Civil War medical kits. ✪ *Map P2* • *Taos Plaza* • *575-758-8545*

10 Tin-Nee-Ann Trading Company
Self-proclaimed "World Famous Tourist Trap" offering wacky knick-knacks. ✪ *Map H5* • *923 Cerrillos Rd* • *505-988-1630*

Chuck Jones Gallery also stocks works by legendary "Peanuts" creator, Charles Schulz.

Left **Sign outside a shop** Center **Red chile pepper, Farmers' Market** Right **Delicious tacos**

🔟 New Mexican Food

1 Traditional Mexican Cuisine

Corn, beans, cheese, tomatoes, and chile are the staples of Mexican cooking. Tortillas, made of ground corn or wheat, are filled with meats, beans, and cheese to form burritos, tacos, or enchiladas. Beans are cooked or fried with lard, or added to the meat and cheese fillings. Usually mild, tomato-based sauces are flavored with chile.

Typical red chile sauce

2 New Mexican Cuisine

Though similar to traditional Mexican, here the sauces are made from freshly ground or dried chiles, rather than tomatoes, and are much hotter. Meals are often accompanied by whole beans or *posole*, made from hominy, lime, pork, chile, garlic, and herbs. *Sopaipillas* are deep-fried breads that are served with honey as a dessert. Some dishes incorporate pine nuts and *tomatillos*, a walnut-sized green berry.

Chile relleno

3 Fusion Cuisine

Many of the area's finest fusion restaurants blend traditional New Mexican cooking with French, Asian, Western, and other international cuisines. The freshest local produce is used in cooking, and often seafood and meats are flown in daily. Chile is a mainstay, providing Southwestern zest to almost every fusion entrée.

4 Burrito

The popular burritos are combinations of beans, meat, cheese, and vegetables wrapped in flour tortillas. Breakfast burritos are a Santa Fe passion and often contain eggs, bacon, sausage, or potatoes. Dinner burritos are larger and served on a plate covered with red or green chile sauce and sides of beans, posole, or rice.

5 Chile Relleno

A whole green chile pepper is stuffed with cheese, dipped in a light egg batter, and then deep fried. The chile is occasionally stuffed with rice or meat.

6 Chiles

Staples of Southwestern sauces and cuisine, chiles are hot peppers that come in a variety of sizes and various degrees of hotness. Santa Fe tends to favor the hotter varieties. Most New Mexican dishes are served with a choice of chile sauces – red,

Santa Fe School of Cooking (505-983-4511) offers cooking classes that focus on Southwestern flavors and ingredients.

Enchiladas with red chile sauce

green, or Christmas, which is both red and green sauce. Green sauce is generally hotter than red sauce, as it is made from fresh chiles. Red sauce is made from dried chiles.

7 Chorizo
Chorizo is a highly spiced Mexican sausage, made with pork and red chile. Although it is often served for breakfast, it is also a staple ingredient of Mexican cooking and is added to soups, stews, and hearty sauces.

8 Enchilada
Rolled or flat corn tortillas are filled or layered with cheese, beef, chicken, or pork, and then baked. They are always topped with chile sauce and cheese. New Mexicans often prefer blue corn tortillas.

9 Huevos Rancheros
A breakfast favorite, fried eggs are served on top of a tortilla and smothered with chile sauce and melted cheese. They are often accompanied with a side of chorizo and beans.

10 Tamale
Ground corn is made into a dough and then filled with finely ground meat, which is often pork, and red chiles. The mixture is then steamed in a corn husk.

Top 10 New Mexican Restaurants

1 La Choza
Authentic chile and classic fare, including tasty enchiladas. ◊ Map L2 • 905 Alarid St, Santa Fe • 505-982-0909 • $$

2 Maria's New Mexican Kitchen
New Mexican food, strolling guitarists, and margaritas. ◊ Map L2 • 555 W Cordova Rd, Santa Fe • 505-983-7929 • $$

3 The Shed
A historic adobe with patio seating. Renowned for its red chile sauce (see p69).

4 Guadalupe Café
Generous portions of flavorful New Mexican dishes. ◊ Map J5 • 422 Old Santa Fe Trail • 505-982-9762 • $$

5 El Patio
Classic New Mexican menu, featuring heart-healthy options (see p101).

6 Diego's Café
Popular for hearty burritos, enchiladas, and icy margaritas (see p77).

7 Casa de Benavidez
Adobe diner with a patio. ◊ Map C6 • 8032 4th St, Albuquerque • 505-898-3311 • $

8 La Placita
New Mexican and American food. ◊ Map P5 • 206 San Felipe St, Albuquerque • 505-247-2204 • $$

9 Orlando's
Typical New Mexican cooking. Try the carne adovada. ◊ Map E2 • 1114 Don Juan Valdez Lane, Taos • 575-751-1450 • $$

10 Guadalajara Grill
Fast self-service, great tacos and enchiladas. ◊ Map E2 • 1384 Paseo del Pueblo Sur, Taos • 575-751-0063 • $

Left **Harry's Roadhouse** Center **Cowgirl BBQ & Western Grill** Right **Bent Street Café & Deli**

🔟 Restaurants

1 Harry's Roadhouse
Generous helpings of creative New Mexican and contemporary cuisine are served in this rambling adobe roadside restaurant. Try the Moroccan stew over couscous and grilled fish tacos. Decadent desserts *(see p85)*.

2 Zia Diner
This stylish Art Deco diner-style restaurant mainly serves meatloaf, fresh roasted turkey, and nightly blue-plate specials. Don't miss the homemade pies, or classic banana split sundae with hot fudge sauce. ✪ *Map G4 • 326 S Guadalupe St, Santa Fe • 505-988-7008 • Dis. access • $$*

3 Café Pasqual's
Easy location, hand-painted murals, and rich Southwestern fare draw a loyal clientele. Dinner fare includes enchiladas and grilled rack of lamb, while the legendary breakfasts feature enormous omelets and other New Mexican favorites *(see p69)*.

4 Artichoke Café
The imaginative menu at this trendy uptown café presents contemporary American, French, and Italian cuisine with a Southwestern touch. Roasted free range chicken with Madeira sauce is a good starter. The wine list is sophisticated *(see p101)*.

5 Michael's Kitchen
Tacos, burgers, sandwiches, salads, and vegetarian enchiladas are served at this busy restaurant with a casual Wild West flair. Its bakery offers New Mexican and American favorites. Breakfast served all day *(see p93)*.

6 Blue Corn Café & Brewery
Delectable New Mexican fare and creative takes on classic pub food are served in this friendly brewpub. The award-winning microbrews are on tap, and the margaritas are frosty. The other branch in Cerrillos Road (505-438-1800) occasionally offers musical evenings *(see p69)*.

Cheerful interior of Café Pasqual

Unless otherwise stated, all restaurants are open daily, accept credit cards, and serve vegetarian dishes.

Entrance, Cowgirl BBQ & Western Grill

7 Cowgirl BBQ & Western Grill

Enjoy generous quantities of barbeque and Southwestern fare in a lovely patio. Attractions include salmon tacos with *tomatillo* sauce and pork chops with a bourbon glaze. Nightly entertainment features blues, rock, or country music *(see p69)*.

8 Bent Street Café & Deli

This bright, cheerful restaurant features an inviting covered patio area and friendly service. Try a simple peanut-butter sandwich, or go for the elegant tiger prawns with sun-dried tomatoes, artichoke hearts, and green-chile pesto *(see p93)*.

9 Cloud Cliff Bakery

The creative menu here offers rainbow trout wraps or black-bean chipotle chile for lunch, and herb-grilled polenta with chile sauce or blue-corn pancakes with granola for breakfast. The in-house bakery sells breads and pastries *(see p85)*.

10 Church Street Café

Dine in the casual elegance of the oldest residence in town, and enjoy New Mexican cuisine with very hot red chile sauce, or select one of the soups and sandwiches *(see p101)*.

Top 10 Gourmet Restaurants

1 Santacafé
Ultra-fresh seafoods and meats *(see p69)*.

2 Geronimo
Gourmet entrées in a romantic setting. ◎ Map L2 • 724 Canyon Rd • 505-982-1500 • Dis. access • $$$$$

3 Fuego
International cuisine, great wines. ◎ Map L4 • 330 E Palace Ave, Santa Fe • 505-954-9670 • Dis. access • $$$$$

4 Old House
Fine dining in a stylish dining room. ◎ Map H3 • 309 W San Francisco St • 505-995-4530 • Partial dis. access • $$$$

5 La Casa Sena
Acclaimed Southwestern cuisine. ◎ Map K4 • 125 E Palace Ave • 505-988-9232 • Partial dis. access • $$$$$

6 Coyote Café
Fine dining, Southwestern style. ◎ Map J4 • 132 W Water St, Santa Fe • 505-983-1615 • Dis. access • $$$$$

7 The Compound
Contemporary American cuisine with a Mediterranean flair. ◎ Map L2 • 653 Canyon Rd, Santa Fe • 505-982-4353 • Partial dis. access • $$$$$

8 The Stakeout
Views of the Sangre de Cristo Mountains, and classic American versions of steaks and seafood *(see p93)*.

9 De La Tierra
Global and regional flavors in a luxurious eco-spa. ◎ Map Q3 • 317 Kit Carson Rd, Taos • 575-737-9855 • Dis. access • $$$$$

10 Doc Martin's
Great ambience, world-class American cuisine, and an excellent wine list *(see p93)*.

For a key to price categories see pp69, 77, 85, 93, 101.

Left **Aromatic oils** Center **Avanyu Spa at La Posada de Santa Fe** Right **SpaTerre at Loretto**

TOP 10 Spas

1 Ten Thousand Waves Japanese Spa

In a lovely mountain setting, this tranquil Japanese-style spa has charmed Santa Fe for more than two decades. Services include Japanese Nightingale facials and Flowing Rivers stone massage. Signature offerings feature the Four Hands, One Heart massage, where two skilled therapists work in unison. ⊛ *Map M1 • 3451 Hyde Park Rd, Santa Fe • 505-992-5025 • www.tenthousandwaves.com*

2 SpaTerre at Inn at Loretto

This elegant spa provides exotic Indonesian experiences, such as the Balinese massage ritual, or a relaxing soak in a flower-strewn tub with aromatic herbs and oils. Skilled therapists go a step further here, with special offerings that can include a gentle massage for mothers-to-be, or couples' massage in a romantic room. ⊛ *Map K4 • 211 Old Santa Fe Trail • 505-984-7997 • Dis. access • www.innatloretto.com*

SpaTerre at Loretto

3 Nidah Spa at El Dorado

Treatments based on Native American traditions are the specialty of this ultra-modern spa. Fresh New Mexican herbs, oils, and plants are used in all spa treatments, including massages, wraps, scrubs, and facials. Other offerings include a Vichy shower, full-service salon, eucalyptus steam rooms, and in-spa lunch service. ⊛ *Map H3 • 309 W San Francisco St, Santa Fe • 505-995-4535 • Dis. access • www.nidahspa.com*

4 Avanyu Spa at La Posada de Santa Fe

This reputed spa offers a wide range of spa treatments and fitness programs. Water therapies incorporate nourishing seaweed and local herbs. Hot-stone massage is their forte, with a variety of New Age treatments. ⊛ *Map L4 • 330 E Palace Ave, Santa Fe • 505-986-0000 • Dis. access • http://laposada.rockresorts.com*

5 El Monte Sagrado Living Spa

Sunlight streams through the high glass ceilings at this spa set amid waterfalls and tropical plants. Treatments available here range from facials and body polishes to custom, hot-stone and deep tissue massages, as well as a complete lineup of New Age therapies. Personal consultations are also available. ⊛ *Map Q3 • 317 Kit Carson Rd, Taos • 575-758-3502 • Dis. access • www.elmontesagrado.com*

6 ShaNah Spa & Wellness at Bishop's Lodge

Set in the foothills of the Sangre de Cristo Mountains, this wellness-oriented spa offers a full range of traditional spa and New Age treatments. Innovative offerings include Ayurvedic rituals tailored to soothe the nervous system. Private outdoor verandas may be reserved.
Ⓢ Map M1 • 1297 Bishop's Lodge Rd, Santa Fe • 505-983-6377 • Dis. access

ShaNah Spa & Wellness at Bishop's Lodge

7 Ojo Caliente Mineral Springs

One of the oldest health resorts in North America, offering seven mineral pools fed by natural geothermal springs. These one-of-a-kind hot springs contain a unique mixture of iron, lithia, soda, arsenic, and sodium, and were visited by ancient Native American tribes long ago. Natural spa treatments are also available, and there are hiking trails nearby. Ⓢ Map D2 • 50 Los Baños Drive, Ojo Caliente • 800-222-9162 • Partial dis. access • www.ojocalientespa.com

8 Tamaya Mist Spa & Salon at Hyatt

This Hyatt-created luxury spa offers meditation and outdoor relaxation areas, as well as a full salon and specialty massages with fresh local herbs. The staff are especially attentive to first-time spa clients, and many treatment rooms have private outdoor patios. Ⓢ Map C5 • 1300 Tuyuna Trail, Santa Ana Pueblo • 505-867-1234 • Dis. access • www.tamaya.hyatt.com

9 Vista Clara Ranch Spa Resort

Recently refurbished, this nationally-renowned destination eco-spa is sprawled across 140 acres. Hot mineral springs and Native American-influenced body treatments are the specialty. A full range of spa, salon, New Age offerings, and personal therapeutic consultations is available. Indulge in a Bones of the Earth Hot-Stone Massage or the Hopi Raindrop Therapy.
Ⓢ Map D5 • Galisteo • 505-466-4772 • www.vistaclara.com

10 Spa Samadhi at The Inn at Sunrise Springs

Tranquil and elegant, this spa offers a range of treatments, as well as yoga and movement options, and traditional arts such as the Japanese tea ceremony. Relax with a signature Hot-Stone Massage, or the Bamboo Lemongrass Polish. Massages for mothers-to-be are also available.
Ⓢ Map D5 • 242 Los Pinos Rd, Santa Fe • 505-471-3600 • Partial dis. access • www.innatsunrisesprings.com

Left **Ballooning** Right **Whitewater rafting**

🔟 Outdoor Activities

1 Ballooning
Endless skies and broad desert plains amid wind-deflecting mountains, have created the perfect conditions for precision ballooning. Ballooning is a year-round activity here, and many local vendors offer ballooning opportunities for visitors.

2 Bicycling
From challenging mountain biking to a casual urban peddle, the area has it all. Mountain bikers head for Santa Fe's Dale Ball trails *(see p75)* or the longer trails through the public lands of the Enchanted Circle *(see p94)*. Santa Fe and Albuquerque have well-marked, in-town bike paths and New Mexico's scenic byways, such as the Turquoise Trail *(see p84)*, offer great touring options.
🔖 www.cabq.gov/bike

3 Bird-Watching
The National Audubon Society has identified 16 great birding areas in Santa Fe and Taos, with walking directions and bird lists. The Rio Grande Nature Center and Sandia Crest *(see p84)* are great birding spots, while the Randall Davy Center is a good choice for shorter outings. 🔖 *Rio Grande Nature Center: Map C6 • 505-344-7240*

4 Hiking
Hiking choices are abundant, from high mountain trails to rocky canyons and high-desert countryside. Well-maintained trails can be found at Bandelier National Monument *(see pp30–31)* and in the stunning public lands of the Enchanted Circle.

5 Horseback Riding
Connect to the Wild West on a trail ride with plenty of local ranches to choose from. Historic Bishop's Lodge *(see p53)* offers guided, private, breakfast, and sunset rides through the Sangre de Cristo Mountains.

6 Golf
Clear desert air and 300 days of sunshine make for great golfing in northern New Mexico. More than a dozen pueblo, resort, and public courses provide variety.
🔖 *Sun Country Amateur Golf Association: Map C6 • 505-897-0864*

A golfer on the green, getting ready to tee off

7 River Rafting
Rio Grande and Rio Chama offer the best whitewater rafting in New Mexico. On the Rio Grande, Taos Box offers thrilling Class 4 rapids, while the Rio Grande Racecourse is Class 3. Season starts in late April, when the rivers are high. By mid-summer, trips become more family-friendly.

The Rio Grande Nature Center offers weekend birding and nature walks as well as walks on full moon nights.

Horseback riding on Ghost Ranch

Rock Climbing
Some of the best rock climbing is found in Taos county. Popular destinations include Dead Cholla Wall, Questa Dome, and Tres Piedras. Both Santa Fe and Albuquerque have indoor climbing gyms as well. *Stone Age Climbing Gym: 4201 Yale NE, Albuquerque; 505-341-2016; www. climbstoneage.com • Santa Fe Climbing Center: Map L2; 505-986-8944; www. climbsantafe.com*

Fishing
Many of the region's rivers, lakes, and streams are filled with German brown and rainbow trout. Fly fishing is extremely popular, and the mountain streams of the Enchanted Circle and the mountains around Taos offer some of America's finest fishing venues. *New Mexico Game and Fish: Map D4 • 800-862-9310*

Skiing
The high-mountain ski areas have plenty of powder snow. Ranked among North America's finest ski resorts is Taos Ski Valley, while Santa Fe Ski Area, and Red River are particularly popular with families. Angel Fire Resort *(see p94)* is the ultimate destination for snowboarders, and the Enchanted Circle offers great opportunities for cross-country skiing.

Top 10 Outdoor Tours

1 Rainbow Ryders
Hot air balloon rides all year. *Map C6 • 505-823-1111 • www.rainbowryders.com*

2 Mellow Velo Bikes
Mountain or desert bike trips. *Map J4 • 505-995-8356 • www.mellowbike.com*

3 National Audubon Society/Randall Davy Audubon Center
Two birding trails and guided nature tours *(see pp12–13).*

4 The Reel Life
Orvis-endorsed fly fishing shop and guide service. *Map G4 • 505-995-8114 • www.reellifesantafe.com*

5 Marty Sanchez Golf Course
Public golf course with 9- and 18-hole courses. Book ahead. *Map D4 • 505-955-4400*

6 Santa Fe Mountain Adventures
Day programs combined with the region's finest spas. *Map J4 • 800-965-4010 • www. santafemountainadventures.com*

7 Broken Saddle Riding Company
Trail rides into Cerrillos mining country. *Map D5 • 505-424-7774 • www.brokensaddle.com*

8 New Wave Rafting Company
Rafting trips on Rio Grande and Rio Chama. *Map L2 • 800-984-1444 • www. newwaverafting.com*

9 Mountain Skills, Rock Climbing Adventures
Guide-led mountain climbing. *Map E2 • 575-776-2222 • www.climbingschoolusa.com*

10 New Mexico Touring Society
Bicycling club with links to hundreds of organized tours. *505-237-9700 • www.nmts.org*

The New Mexico PLIC (505-438-7542) has maps and activity information on New Mexico's best trails.

Left & center left **Explora!** Center right **Exhibit, Museum of International Folk Art** Right **Polar bear**

Children's Attractions

1 Explora!

At this interactive learning museum, children can create dams and lakes at the water-table, change the direction of wind to shape sand dunes, or direct balls through a giant three-dimensional maze of color.
⊗ Map P5 • 1701 Mountain Rd NW, Albuquerque • 505-224-8300 • Open 10am–6pm Mon–Sat, noon–6pm Sun • Adm • www.explora.mus.nm.us

2 Santa Fe Children's Museum

Children enjoy the diversity this museum offers. They can scale a climbing wall, build bridges with giant magnets, create art from recycled materials, or explore nature. Special programs bring in artists and scientists to guide children through hands-on activities. ⊗ Map L2 • 1050 Old Pecos Trail • 505-989-8359 • Open 10am–5pm Wed–Sat, noon–5pm Sun • Adm • Partial dis. access • www.santafechildrensmuseum.org

3 Anderson-Abruzzo International Balloon Museum

This exceptional museum helps children discover how a balloon flies and learn about the soldiers, adventurers, and spies who have used balloons. In fine weather, they can even soar aloft in a tethered hot-air balloon. A "virtual balloon ride" takes them over the splendid desert landscape of New Mexico (see p98).

Skeleton of a dinosaur

4 New Mexico Museum of Natural History and Science

High-tech exhibits and realistic special effects make learning about New Mexico's natural history fun for everyone. Walk across a river of hot bubbling lava into an erupting volcano. Explore a bat-filled cave or step into the "Evolution Elevator", to be transported back to the age of dinosaurs. The volunteers enjoy answering questions about the natural world (see p97).

Museum of International Folk Art

5 Albuquerque Rio Grande Zoo

The zoo's popular exhibits include big cats and polar bears. The aquarium-like windows allow you to watch the bears as they swim underwater. Other favorites are the bat enclosure and the reptile house with its collection of rattlesnakes. A petting zoo operates in the summer *(see p98)*.

Aquarium, Albuquerque BioPark

6 American International Rattlesnake Museum

More than six of the largest rattlesnake collections in the world are displayed at this conservation-oriented museum. The different species of live rattlesnakes are kept in recreated habitats, and the exhibits are extremely informative. Favorites include Marilyn, a rare albino western diamondback rattlesnake, and Ramona, a mottled rock rattlesnake with camouflage coloring *(see p43)*.

American International Rattlesnake Museum

7 Bandelier National Monument

Children love climbing the short, sturdy ladders to explore the ancient pueblo cave dwellings that dot the cliff face. The Frijoles Canyon Trail provides Indian ruins and cliff dwellings along a one-hour walk *(see pp30–31)*.

8 Tinkertown Museum

A delightful, fun and inspirational museum. With a push of a button, the wonderfully comical, hand-carved figures of the Wild West and circus "villages" come to life. The Old Geezer's chair rocks, Susie jumps rope, and the wagon moves *(see p82)*.

9 Museum of International Folk Art

Children always love the brightly-colored folk art toys and objects that fill this captivating museum. There are vividly painted dolls from Morocco, West Africa, and Italy; a jaguar mask from Mexico, a deer mask from Guatemala; and birds, leopards, horses, and cats made with paper, wood or clay *(see p81)*.

10 Albuquerque BioPark

For many children, the ultimate experience at this exceptional city aquarium is watching the divers at work in a huge tank filled with sleek, menacing sharks. Elsewhere, floor-to-ceiling glass walls offer splendid views into watery worlds brimming with tropical fish and a stunning array of marine life. At the Botanic Gardens, you can watch the train that rolls through the gardens next to the aquarium *(see p98)*.

Left **Christmas in Santa Fe** Center **Native American dancers** Right **A craftsman at work**

Festivals and Events

Gathering of Nations
North America's largest Pow Wow attracts Native American dancers from hundreds of tribes across Canada and the US. Native arts and crafts are displayed at the Indian Traders' Market. ⊗ *Map C6 • University of New Mexico Arena • Apr • Adm • www.gatheringofnations.com*

Rodeo de Santa Fe
One of the nation's top 100 rodeos attracts rodeo stars, with bronc riding, steer wrestling, and calf roping events, as well as a parade through the streets. ⊗ *Map D5 • 3237 Rodeo Rd • 505-471-4300 • Jun • Adm • www.rodeosantafe.com*

Spring Festival El Rancho de las Golondrinas
A living history festival, with costumed re-enactors playing the roles of villagers. Expect festive dances and music, an outdoor mass, and food *(see pp28–9)*. ⊗ *Map D5 • Jun • Adm*

Taos Pueblo Pow Wow
Native American dancers from tribes across North America come to Taos Pueblo for this annual event. The Grand Entrance is spectacular, as costumed dancers circle the field. ⊗ *Map E2 • 505-758-1028 • Jul • Adm • www. taospueblopowwow.com*

Pow Wow dancer

Spanish Market
Major Southwestern Hispanic arts event, attracting international collectors and art enthusiasts, with religious carvings and paintings, embroidery, textiles, tinwork, and pine furniture. ⊗ *Map J4 • Santa Fe Plaza • 505-982-2226 • Late Jul & early Dec • www.spanishcolonial.org*

Indian Market
The world's most respected Native American arts event features more than 1,200 of the country's best Native American artists and craftspeople. Food booths offer authentic traditional Native American cuisine. ⊗ *Map J4 • Santa Fe Plaza • 505-983-5220 • Aug (third weekend) • www.swaia.org*

Santa Fe Fiesta
The nation's oldest community celebration and Santa Fe's largest festival mark de Vargas's *(see p34)* 1692 victory and the Spanish reoccupation of Santa Fe. A fun-filled weekend of colorful parades, parties, mariachi music, and activities begins Friday evening with the burning of Zozóbra, or Old Man Gloom, ushering in the positive for the next year. ⊗ *Map J4 • Santa Fe Plaza • Sep (weekend after Labor Day) • www.santafefiesta.org*

Pot for sale, Indian Market

Albuquerque International Balloon Fiesta

In the world's largest ballooning event, highlights include the evening Balloon Glow, where tethered balloons fire their burners and light up the night sky. Booths offer food and an array of balloon merchandise, and professional tour operators offer hot-air balloon rides. • Map C6 • 505-821-1000 • Early Oct • Adm • www.balloonfiesta.com

Harvest Festival El Rancho de las Golondrinas

Costumed interpreters crush grapes for wine, grind corn and wheat in a water-powered mill, and string fiery red chile *ristras*. Festivities center around bringing in the autumn harvest. Craft demonstrations include leather, woodworking, and wool weaving. • Map D5 • Oct • www. golondrinas.org

Corn for grinding

Christmas in Santa Fe

Thousands of *farolitas* (small lanterns) fill the Plaza area and Canyon Road. Festivities occur at the Palace of the Governors, and the traditional outdoor Spanish play *Las Posadas* is performed on the Plaza. Events also include ceremonial dances at the pueblos, and holiday music at the historic churches. • www.santafe.org

Top 10 Music Events

1 Taos Chamber Music Festival
Taos School of Music concert series. • 575-776-2388 • Mid-Jun–early Aug • Adm • www.taosschoolofmusic.com

2 Summer Nights
Country, folk, and bluegrass music in the Albuquerque Botanic Gardens. • Thu eve, Jun–mid-Aug

3 Santa Fe Chamber Music Festival
Events of fine ensemble music. • 505-983-2075 • Mid-Jul–mid-Aug • Adm • www.sfcmf.org

4 Santa Fe Opera
Five world class operas in a beautiful open-air opera house (see p74). • Jul & Aug

5 Desert Chorale
A wide range of music performed in historic churches. • 505-988-2282 • Jul & Aug • Adm • www.desertchorale.org

6 Maria Benitez Teatro Flamenco
Flamenco by a notable troupe. • 505-955-8562 • Jul & Aug • Adm • www.mariabenitez.com

7 Music from Angel Fire
Chamber music by international artists. • 505-989-4772 • Mid-Aug–early Sep • Adm

8 Santa Fe Symphony Orchestra and Chorus
Seven concerts presented each year. • 505-983-1414 • Oct–Apr • Adm • www.sf-symphony.org

9 New Mexico Symphony Orchestra
Multi-cultural performances throughout the year. • 505-881-9590 • www.nmso.org

10 Albuquerque Little Theatre
Comedy, musicals, and drama throughout the year. • 505-242-4750 • www.albuquerquelittletheatre.org

AROUND SANTA FE, TAOS, & ALBUQUERQUE

Left **St. Francis Cathedral** Center **Morning Star Gallery** Right **Chapel, Palace of the Governors**

Central Santa Fe

THE CENTER OF "THE CITY DIFFERENT" *is the historic crossroads of the Wild West, the meeting point of two great roads – El Camino Real and the Santa Fe Trail – and a rich melting pot of Native, Anglo, and Hispanic cultures. Today, art buyers, history enthusiasts, and connoisseurs of food congregate here to sample the best of Santa Fe. The Plaza is at its heart, once the hub of traders, adventurers, and outlaws, now it bustles with tourists. Surrounding the Plaza are 20 or more blocks of narrow streets lined with historic adobe buildings that contain a mind-boggling array of museums, cafés, shops of every description, and some of the finest dining choices in America. More than 200 magnificent galleries offer fine art of every style and description, from traditional Western masterpieces to cutting-edge works of the 21st century.*

🔟 Sights

1. Palace of the Governors
2. Shops and Galleries
3. Santa Fe Plaza
4. Native Portal
5. Canyon Road
6. Georgia O'Keeffe Museum
7. Loretto Chapel
8. La Fonda Hotel Lobby
9. St. Francis Cathedral
10. Institute of American Indian Arts Museum

Native Americans selling jewelry

Preceding pages: **Holy Cross Catholic Church**

Palace of the Governors
Built in 1610 as the seat of government for the huge Spanish Colonial territory of New Mexico, this building served as the center of regional power for over 300 years. Inside, the rooms contain artifacts, photographs, and furnishings that tell the fascinating history of New Mexico. Take one of the tours led by the superbly trained docents, and don't miss the Bland Mud Wagon, the Segesser Hide Paintings, and the Palace Press, a working historic printing office. ◎ Map K3 • 105 W Palace Ave • 505-476-5100 • Open 10am–5pm Tue–Sun • Adm • Dis. access

Shops and Galleries
Santa Fe is the ultimate shopper's paradise, with narrow historic roads lined with a surfeit of art galleries and shops. There are also many one-of-a-kind boutiques offering a wide variety of art, jewelry, clothing, and gifts. Look for unique creative shops such as the Back at the Ranch (see p66) that sells a dazzling array of handmade cowboy boots. The maze-like wonderland of Asian rugs and furniture at Seret & Sons is a must-visit (see p66). Also worth a look are the museum shops selling art, books, and souvenirs.

Cowboy boot for sale, Back at the Ranch

Santa Fe Plaza
Since 1610, the Plaza has been a popular place to socialize, walk the paths, or sit on the benches to watch the ebb and flow of activity in the nearby streets lined with restaurants, shops, galleries, and museums. At Christmas, it is lined with candle-lit farolitas, and several times a year art shows and festivals are held here. ◎ Map J4

A scenic view of Santa Fe Plaza

Native Portal
One of the best places to buy Native American jewelry and art in the Southwest, the Native Portal gives you a chance to meet the artists and learn about jewelry. The Museum of New Mexico has established stringent quality and manufacturing requirements. If you like a piece, but aren't ready to buy it, ask for contact details, as the next day there will be different artists here. ◎ Map J3

Canyon Road
One of the most renowned art buying destinations in the world, the mile-long ramble along this colorful winding lane is a delight for veteran art lovers and novices alike. Over 80 galleries offer the finest works of every imaginable variety. Sculptures adorn flower-filled courtyards, and ornate fountains grace lovely garden nooks. Several fine dining restaurants and cafés offer respite and refreshment from the walk, and on Friday evenings the galleries stay open late and the street comes alive as musicians and street performers entertain (see pp12–13).

Santa Fe Style

Starting in 1912, Santa Fe passed adobe-only building codes that mandated that all new construction employ either Pueblo Revival or Territorial architectural styles. The intent was to create a visually unified community, and to increase tourism. The Territorial-style buildings designed by John Gaw Meem typify the Santa Fe "look".

Georgia O'Keeffe Museum

Dedicated to New Mexico's most famous resident artist, Georgia O'Keeffe, this museum has a large collection of her paintings, drawings, and sculptures. In 2006, the Georgia O'Keeffe Foundation donated more than 1,000 of her drawings, paintings, sculptures, and materials to the museum. The museum also owns O'Keeffe's home and studio in Abiquiu, and her Ghost Ranch property, offering a limited number of tours annually *(see pp14–15)*.

Loretto Chapel

Although the "Miraculous Staircase" *(see p44)* is the best-known feature of this charming Gothic chapel, it is a beautiful space with a lovely nave and altar. Designed by Projectus Mouly, son of Antoine Mouly who was the architect of St. Francis Cathedral, it was the chapel of the nuns of Loretto.

The most renowned of the nuns was the niece of Archbishop Lamy. Born in France, she entered the Loretto novitiate, becoming Sister Francesca.
Map K4 • 277 Old Santa Fe Trail • 505-982-0092 • Open summer: 9am–6pm; winter: 9am–4.30pm Mon–Sat, 10:30am–5pm Sun (all year) • Adm • Dis. access

La Fonda Hotel Lobby

From 1926 to 1969, La Fonda was one of the finest of the hotels known as Harvey Houses. The Atchison, Topeka, & Santa Fe Railroad owned the hotel, and leased it to Fred Harvey, who was often credited with opening the West to tourism. Harvey hired Mary Colter, one of the most prominent woman architects of the 20th century, to design the hotel's interior. Working with the Pueblo-style Spanish architecture, featuring huge wooden beams, *latilla* ceilings, and carved corbels, Colter hired local artisans to create many of the artistic details, including the decorative tin and copper light fixtures. In the 1920s, Gerald Cassidy was commissioned to paint 10 portraits, including *Kit Carson* and *Spanish Dancer*, which still adorn the lobby near the front desk. The artwork-filled lobby and hallways enhance La Fonda's fame as one of Santa Fe's favorite meeting places. *Map K4 • 100 E San Francisco St • 505-982-5511*

Inside Georgia O'Keeffe Museum

Call the Georgia O'Keeffe Museum before you go, and if it is closed take more time to explore the Museum of Fine Arts see p41.

Gothic Loretto Chapel

St. Francis Cathedral

9 Archbishop Lamy employed French designers and Italian stonemasons to plan the Cathedral Basilica of St. Francis of Assisi. The rose window in front and the lateral nave windows came from Clermont-Ferrand, France, and were installed in 1884. A century later, New Mexico *santero*-style Stations of the Cross were added along the nave. The statue of St. Francis was added in 1967.
Ⓢ *Map K4 • 131 Cathedral Pl • 505-982-5619 • Open 6.30am–5.45pm daily • Dis. access*

Institute of American Indian Arts Museum

10 This museum has a remarkable collection of over 7,000 pieces of contemporary Native American art. Many of the works on display are by former graduates of the institute, and you will also find students working in the museum. The museum shop is full of fascinating and attractive pieces, including work by the students. The campus is also open to the public who are welcome to tour the facilities.
Ⓢ *Map K4 • 108 Cathedral Pl • 505-983-1777 • Open 10am–5pm Mon–Sat, noon–5pm Sun, closed major hols*

A Day Around Santa Fe

Morning

Start in front of **St. Francis Cathedral** and step inside to marvel at the stained-glass windows and the French-Romanesque architecture. Walk down East San Francisco Street and enter **La Fonda**. Explore the shops, admire the artwork in the lobby and the painted windows around the restaurant. Walk outdoors and turn left on to East San Francisco Street and continue to historic **Santa Fe Plaza** *(see p63)*.

Cross the Plaza to shop for Native American jewelry under the **Portal** *(see p63)* of the **Palace of the Governors** *(see p63)*. Inside, join a docent tour to learn about the rich history of Santa Fe and New Mexico. When you leave, turn left and follow East Palace Avenue to **The Shed** *(see p69)* for lunch.

Afternoon

After lunch take in some of the exhibits of the **Institute of American Indian Arts Museum** or wander around its fine campus. Then walk back past the Palace of the Governors and cross Lincoln Avenue to enter the **Museum of Fine Arts** *(see p41)*. Enjoy the fine exhibits of traditional and contemporary art. Continue down West Palace Avenue to Grant Avenue and turn right. At the pedestrian crossing, cross left on to Johnson Street. **The Georgia O'Keeffe Museum** is on the right. Stop in the museum to view the newest exhibit and enjoy the vibrant colors of O'Keeffe's famous paintings of flowers and landscapes.

Left **Back at the Ranch** Right **Simply Santa Fe**

Galleries and Shops

Gerald Peters Gallery
One of Santa Fe's best-known galleries displays works from the previous centuries, as well as contemporary art. § Map L5 • 1011 Paseo de Peralta • 505-954-5700 • Dis. access • www.gpgallery.com

Morning Star Gallery
Masterpieces of Native American art are housed in this museum-quality gallery. § Map M5 • 513 Canyon Rd • 505-982-8187 • Dis. access • www.morningstargallery.com

Seret & Sons
Colorful items from Tibet to Peru include modern and antique rugs, fanciful furniture, carved statues, and handcrafted doors. § Map J4 • 224 Galisteo St • 505-988-9151 • Partial dis. access

Nedra Matteucci Galleries
Rare works by American Western, Impressionist, Modern, and leading contemporary artists. § Map L6 • 1075 Paseo de Peralta • 505-982-4631 • Partial dis. access • www.matteucci.com

Packards on the Plaza
Renowned for traditional and contemporary Native American jewelry, pottery, accessories, and Navajo and Pueblo weavings. § Map J4 • 61 Old Santa Fe Trail • 505-983-9241 • Dis. access

The Rainbow Man
Since 1945, this delightful adobe-walled alleyway shop has been selling Mexican pottery, blankets, folk art, vintage jewelry, and ceramics. § Map K4 • 107 E Palace Ave • 505-982-8706 • Partial dis. access

Back at the Ranch
This bright boutique offers a fascinating selection of handmade cowboy boots and accessories. § Map L3 • 209 E Marcy St • 505-989-8110 • Dis. access

Kiva Fine Art
This gallery celebrates 21st-century Native American art. The displays include traditional and contemporary sculpture, rugs and paintings. § Map J4 • 102 E Water St • 505-820-7413 • www.kivaindianart.com

Handwoven Originals
Local artist-weavers create handwoven apparel, while jewelry and accessories are crafted by a group of regional artists. § Map K4 • 211 Old Santa Fe Trail • 505-982-4118

Simply Santa Fe
Stocks home furnishings, Old Hickory Tannery Western furniture, and bedding and linens by Daniel Stuart Studio. § Map J4 • 72 E San Francisco St • 505-988-3100 • Dis. access

Galleries and shops are usually open daily, though some may be closed on Mondays, weekends, or holidays. Call for timings.

Left **A horno** Center **Portal, Taos Plaza** Right **Typical adobe structure with blue door**

🔟 Aspects of Santa Fe Architecture

1 Traditional Adobe
These are buildings formed with sun-dried bricks of earth and water. The Spanish added straw for greater stability. The walls of the house are annually coated with clay. Stunning Taos Pueblo *(see pp22–3)* is the best example.

2 Pueblo Revival
Modeled after the traditional homes of Pueblo Indians, these cube or rectangular buildings have flat roofs, adobe or stucco walls, rounded corners, and small windows. The Museum of Fine Arts *(see p41)* is an excellent example.

3 Territorial Style
This modified Pueblo Revival style has several additional features such as rows of brick at the roofline, a broad central hallway and entryway, and broad roofed portal. The Museum of Spanish Colonial Art *(see p81)* is a classic example.

4 Viga
A horizontal roof beam made from a large log, which usually extends through the exterior wall and is visible from the outside. A single layer of beams is used in a building, so the *vigas* show on just two of its sides.

5 Corbel
An ornately carved, wooden angular bracket originally placed at the junction of vertical posts and horizontal beams.

6 Blue Doors and Windows
Throughout the region, many doors and widows are painted in fetching shades of blue and blue-green. The colors not only accent the earthy tones of adobe, but are also believed to protect the house and its occupants from evil spirits.

7 Portal
A covered walkway or porch designed to offer protection from the sun and rain. Portals are sometimes incorporated into a building with heavy adobe arches, or feature roofs supported by strong uprights made of logs or heavy timbers.

8 Walled Courtyard
The courtyard walls are usually built with adobe to provide a private patio and garden space. Sometimes a coyote fence, vertical branches wired together, is used instead of adobe.

9 Kiva Fireplace
An interior adobe fireplace, usually located in the corner of the room. The rounded shape resembles that of a Native American ceremonial kiva. Their practical beauty has made them a chic addition to modern homes.

10 Horno
An outdoor domed oven built with adobe, that is used to bake bread and other goods. These ovens were introduced by the Spanish colonists and later adopted by the Pueblo Indians.

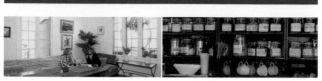

Left **The Teahouse** Right **Aztec Café**

🔟 Cafés and Coffee Shops

1 Zélé Café
Arty gem, serving light meals and fresh roasted coffees. Inside seating and a large outdoor patio area. ◈ *Map J4 • 201 Galisteo St • 505-982-7835 • Dis. access*

2 The Teahouse
A selection of 100 loose teas from around the world, desserts, scones, soups, salads, and sandwiches. ◈ *Map L2 • 821 Canyon Rd • 505-992-0972 • Partial dis. access*

3 Aztec Café
Try the sandwiches made with fresh bagels and bakery bread. There are also many teas and coffees to choose from. ◈ *Map H4 • 317 Aztec St • 505-820-0025*

4 Downtown Subscription
Browse through a variety of magazines and newspapers, or step up to the coffee bar for a choice of imported blends and pastries. ◈ *Map L6 • 376 Garcia St • 505-983-3085 • Dis. access*

5 Travel Bug
The collection of maps and guidebooks is staggering, and the house blend java is hearty. Free high-speed wireless Internet. ◈ *Map L4 • 839 Paseo de Peralta • 505-992-0418*

6 Café Dominic
Chef Dominic Romero incorporates local ingredients in breakfast, lunch, and dinner specialities. ◈ *Map G4 • 320 S Guadalupe St • 505-982-4743*

7 O'Hori's Coffee
Enjoy coffee roasted on the premises at this café, with a gift shop selling chocolates and 30 varieties of coffee. ◈ *Map J4 • 507 Old Santa Fe Trail • 505-988-7026*

8 El Cañon Wine and Coffee Bar
A cozy place for cappuccino, latte, and espresso. Muffins, hand-carved sandwiches, stew, soups, and salads also feature. Fine wines, specialty brews, and cocktails available as well. ◈ *Map H3 • 100 Sandoval St • 505-986-6417*

9 Santa Fe Baking Co. & Café
Bustling local coffee shop and bakery. Smoothie bar, free Wi-Fi. ◈ *Map L2 • 504 W Cordova Rd • 505-988-4292*

10 CD Café
Curl up on a comfortable couch to enjoy a wide range of espresso and other drinks, as well as light snacks. Check out the new and used CDs that you can listen to before buying. ◈ *Map G2 • 301 N Guadalupe St • 505-986-0735*

Unless otherwise stated, all cafés are open daily.

Price Categories

For a three-course meal for one, with half a bottle of wine (or equivalent meal), including taxes and extra charges.

$	under $20
$$	$20–40
$$$	$40–55
$$$$	$55–80
$$$$$	over $80

Above **Interior, 315 Restaurant & Wine Bar**

🔟 Restaurants

1 Café Pasqual's
The often-changing menu features a fusion of flavors from Old Mexico, New Mexico, and Asia. ◉ Map J4 • 121 Don Gaspar Ave • Partial dis. access • 505-983-9340 • $$$

2 The Shed
Housed in a 1692 adobe, this eatery offers hearty Southwestern cuisine. The desserts are just as famous as the signature extra-hot red sauce. ◉ Map K4 • 113½ E Palace Ave • 505-982-9030 • Closed Sun • $$

3 Santacafé
Set in an 1850s hacienda, this acclaimed restaurant serves a fine blend of New Mexican, Asian, and European cuisines. ◉ Map K3 • 231 Washington Ave • 505-984-1788 • Partial dis. access • $$$$

4 315 Restaurant & Wine Bar
French-provincial menu, a long wine list, nightly specials, and patio dining. ◉ Map K5 • 315 Old Santa Fe Trail • 505-986-9190 • Partial dis. access • $$$

5 Anasazi Restaurant
Innovative global cuisine, featuring organic produce, free range meats, and fresh fish. ◉ Map K3 • 113 Washington Ave • 505-988-3236 • Partial dis. access • $$$$

6 Cowgirl BBQ & Western Grill
Mesquite-smoked barbeque. Next door, the Cowgirl Pickup offers takeout meals. ◉ Map G4 • 319 S Guadalupe St • 505-982-2565 • $$

7 Il Vicino
The wood-fired pizza is superb at this order-at-the-counter restaurant. Compose your own pizza from 25 topping options. ◉ Map H3 • 321 W San Francisco St • 505-986-8700 • Dis. access • $$

8 La Boca
Small and cheerful, this restaurant offers Mediterranean cuisine, with tapas, dishes from southern Spain, and homemade pasta. ◉ Map K3 • 72 W Marcy St • 505-982-4344 • $$

9 Blue Corn Café & Brewery
Spacious and comfortable, this popular lunch spot serves hearty and flavorful New Mexican and pub food. ◉ Map J4 • 133 W Water St • 505-984-1800 • Dis. access • $$

10 Tomasita's Santa Fe Station
Large and tasty portions of New Mexican food. Frozen margaritas, imported beers, and patio seating. ◉ Map G5 • 500 S Guadalupe St • 505-983-5721 • Closed Sun • Partial dis. access • $$

 Unless otherwise stated, all restaurants are open daily, accept credit cards, and serve vegetarian dishes.

Left **A view of Dale Ball Trail** Center **Bradbury Science Museum** Right **Santuario de Chimayó**

Santa Fe North

THE AREA TO THE NORTH OF SANTA FE *includes some of the city's wealthiest suburbs, the world-class Santa Fe Opera, and an abundance of scenic, historic, artistic, and scientific destinations. Tesuque is a charming village nestled in a green valley with fine galleries and sculpture gardens. The High Road to Taos is renowned for the healing powers of the Santuario de Chimayó, and the Spanish artistic traditions of weaving and woodcarving. A second scenic road trip leads to the ancient Pueblo ruins at Bandelier National Monument, and then on to the Los Alamos Bradbury Science Museum. The road leads along the rim of an ancient volcano offering vistas across one of the largest volcanic calderas in the world.*

Left **Church of San Francisco de Asis** Right **A panoramic view of Tesuque village**

🔟 Sights

1. Bandelier National Monument
2. Church of San Francisco de Asis
3. Bradbury Science Museum
4. Tesuque
5. Santa Fe Opera
6. Santa Fe Ski Area
7. Truchas
8. Valles Caldera National Preserve
9. Dale Ball Trails
10. Santuario de Chimayó

Preceding pages: **Santa Fe Opera**

Detail of altarpiece, Church of San Francisco de Asis

1 Bandelier National Monument

This fascinating site contains ruins of villages occupied by Ancestral Pueblo peoples between the 12th and 16th centuries. The paved self-guided Main Loop Trail meanders through Frijoles Canyon past the ancient ceremonial kivas and the huge circular streamside village of Tyuonyi. Serious hikers can take the Falls Trail past two dramatic waterfalls to the Rio Grande River. The Falls Trail is narrow and steep in places, and takes several hours to complete *(see pp30–31)*.

2 Church of San Francisco de Asis

Since the early 1900s, artists and photographers have been inspired by the graceful, hand-built adobe walls of this beautiful Mission church. The pretty front, with its double bell towers and flower-filled meditation garden, makes a lovely place to relax. ◈ *Map E2 • Hwy 68, Rancho de Taos • 575-758-2754 • Open 9am–4pm Mon–Sat • Partial dis. access*

3 Bradbury Science Museum

This outstanding museum traces the history of the Manhattan Project and the development of "Little Boy" and "Fat Man", the first atomic bombs. Many of the projects featured are controversial, and the interactive exhibits present a thought-provoking view of the political, social, and practical complexity of the use of atomic power in science, defense, and weapons. Other displays focus on the ongoing research at the laboratory, including the challenge of maintenance and reliability testing of existing nuclear weapons, now that live testing has been banned ◈ *Map C4 • 15th St & Central Ave, Los Alamos • 505-667-4444 • Open 10am–5pm Tue–Sat, 1pm–5pm Sun–Mon • Dis. access • www.lanl.gov/museum*

4 Tesuque

One of the loveliest small towns near Santa Fe, Tesuque is nestled in a green, tree-shaded valley along a sparkling river. Years ago, artists began arriving, establishing their studios and galleries. The Tesuque Village Market *(see p77)*, the favorite gathering spot, offers meals-to-go, bakery, fresh produce, wines, and gourmet groceries. Tesuque is also home to the popular Shidoni Foundry, Galleries, and Sculpture Garden *(see p76)*. ◈ *Map D4*

5 Santa Fe Opera

This exquisite partially open-air theater presents five operas every summer. Each season's program offers innovative shows of popular classics, less performed masterpieces, and new operas. The modern 2,126-seat amphitheater has excellent acoustics, and the seats have built-in instant-translation screens available in English and Spanish. Pre-performance buffets and tailgate picnics are very popular. Though most performances sell out well in advance, standing-room-only tickets are frequently available on performance day. ◎ Map D4 • US 84/285, 5 miles (8 km) N of Santa Fe • 505-986-5900 • Open Jul & Aug • Dis. access • www.santafeopera.org

Under the roof of the Santa Fe Opera

6 Santa Fe Ski Area

New Mexico's highest ski peak rises over 12,000 ft (4,000 m). With 44 runs, 1,600 ft (488 m) of vertical drop, and short queues, the skiing is great. There are trails to suit every level of skier, from beginner to advanced. A cross-country trail is nearby. The area offers many restaurants, equipment rentals, and package deals. ◎ Map E4 • End of NM 475/Hyde Park Rd • 505-982-4429 • Open late Nov–early Apr • www.skisantafe.com

Art Along the High Road to Taos

The length of the High Road to Taos is dotted with villages with a traditional Spanish Colonial character. Long renowned for their arts, notably Chimayó for its fine wool weaving and Cordova for religious woodcarving, these once isolated villages today have many artist studios and galleries in their midst.

7 Truchas

Founded in 1754 by a 15,000-acre land grant, Truchas retains much of its Spanish village heritage. It was the setting of Robert Redford's movie *The Milagro Beanfield War* in 1986. The pastoral beauty of the valley has drawn newcomers to the village. The art galleries and gift shops are strung along the main road, which continues through the valley, past small farms. Spectacular mountain views and the quiet countryside make for one of the loveliest drives in the area. ◎ Map E3

8 Valles Caldera National Preserve

This awesome crater was formed by a massive volcanic eruption more than a million years ago. The collapsed crater is more than 12 miles (19 km) across, and the meadow-like expanse was used as a huge ranch until the year 2000, when it was purchased by the Federal government and turned into a limited access reserve. The scenic drive from Los Alamos through the Jemez Mountains along State Highway 4 leads along the rim of the caldera, offering overlooks with stunning vistas across the valley. ◎ Map C4 • State Highway 4 • 877-851-8946 • www.vallescaldera.gov

Advance reservations are required to enter Valles Caldera National Preserve, which offers a variety of guided tours and special events.

9 Dale Ball Trails

With 20 miles (32 km) of public hiking and mountain biking routes, this network of trails is one of the best in the nation. There are lovely views back toward Santa Fe and, from higher elevations, out over the open desert and the surrounding mountains. The paths are well marked and maintained, and there are maps at the trailheads and at major intersections along the trail. Take plenty of water and snacks, for none are available along the trails. ◈ Map L2, M2

10 Santuario de Chimayó

Thousands of pilgrims walk to Santuario de Chimayó each year during the Holy Week before Easter Sunday. Native American legends regarding the healing power of this spot pre-date the arrival of Spanish settlers in the late 1600s. The chapel was built by a local landowner in 1814–16 after he experienced a vision. A large cross, found on the site when the chapel was built, is believed to have belonged to martyred priests. Today, visitors are allowed to take home with them some of the miraculous earth from the place of the healing spring. ◈ Map D3 • Chimayó village, on CR 94C • 505-351-4889 • Open 9am–5pm daily

Santuario de Chimayó

Hiking, Hot Tubbing, and Galleries

Morning

🕐 To reach the parking lot at the trailhead of **Dale Ball Trails**, drive northeast on Artist Road/ Hyde Park Road to Sierra del Norte. Turn left, then turn right into the parking lot. After studying the trail map at the north side of the lot, head out for hiking through this lovely mountain terrain. The trail offers alternating views of Santa Fe below, high desert country, and mountain vistas. Returning, exit the parking lot and turn left onto Hyde Park Road, continuing northeast until you reach **Ten Thousand Waves** (see p52), Santa Fe's popular Japanese-style day spa, at 3451 Hyde Park Road. Register for an hour-long soak in a hot tub, choosing either a private or a communal tub. Swimsuits are optional, and the lodge supplies robes, sandals, towels, and shower rooms. Returning to your car, drive back toward Santa Fe on Hyde Park Road. Turn right on Bishop's Lodge Road continuing to NM 590 and **Tesuque Village Market** (see p77) for lunch.

Afternoon

Drive back toward Santa Fe on Bishop's Lodge Road for a few blocks and turn in at the popular **Shidoni Foundry, Galleries, and Sculpture Garden** (see p76). Walk in the garden and admire the unique range of sculpture. Stop in at the galleries, and then walk next door to visit **Tesuque Glassworks** (see p76), where you can watch the glassblowers at work, before heading back to Santa Fe.

Left **Centinela Traditional Arts** Center **The High Road Marketplace** Right **Shidoni Sculpture Garden**

Galleries and Shops

1 Shidoni Foundry, Galleries, and Sculpture Garden
One of the largest selections of contemporary and traditional sculpture in the Western US. ✆ *Map M1 • 1508 Bishop's Lodge Rd • 505-988-8001 • www.shidoni.com*

2 Chimayó Trading and Mercantile
Traditional Native American and Spanish artworks by some of the region's best contemporary artists. ✆ *Map D3 • NM 76, Chimayó • 505-351-4566 • Partial dis. access • www.chimayoarts.com*

3 Ortega's Weaving Shop
For nine generations, the Ortegas have produced hand-woven woolen items. ✆ *Map D3 • NM 76, Chimayó • 505-351-4215 • Dis. access • www.ortegasweaving.com*

4 The High Road Marketplace
Co-op gallery of fine arts and crafts, created in the mountain villages along the High Road to Taos. ✆ *Map D3 • Off CR 98, Chimayó • 505-351-1078 • www.highroadnewmexico.com*

5 Cordovas Handweaving Workshop
Fine-quality contemporary rugs and tapestries, created on a traditional loom. ✆ *Map E3 • CR 75, Truchas Village • 505-689-1124*

6 Tesuque Glassworks
This amazing gallery and glassblowing studio displays fine-art glass and jewelry created on-site. ✆ *Map M1 • 1510 Bishop's Lodge Rd • 505-988-2165*

7 Centinela Traditional Arts
Famed tapestry gallery, specializing in handwoven wool fabrics by master weavers. ✆ *Map D3 • NM 76, Chimayó • 505-351-2180 • www.chimayoweavers.com*

8 Ojo Sarco Pottery
Local artists create exquisite pottery with a petroglyph-like design. Porcelain, glass, textiles, and jewelry are impressive. ✆ *Map E3 • NM 76, Ojo Sarco • 505-689-2354 • www.ojosarco.com*

9 Hand Artes Gallery and Sculpture Garden
Sculptures, paintings, and folk art fill up this delightful place. ✆ *Map E3 • Main Truchas Rd • 505-689-2443*

10 Glenn Green Galleries and Sculpture Garden
Contemporary art gallery, stocking fine bronze sculptures, paintings, rainforest baskets, and ceramics. ✆ *Map D4 • 136 Tesuque Village Rd • 505-820-0008 • www.glenngreengalleries.com*

Chimayó Trading and Mercantile

Many of the galleries and shops are owned by artists or Native Americans, and do not have standard hours. Call for timings.

Price Categories

For a three-course meal for one, with half a bottle of wine (or equivalent meal), including taxes and extra charges.

$	under $20
$$	$20–40
$$$	$40–55
$$$$	$55–80
$$$$$	over $80

Above **Buzzing interior of Tesuque Village Market**

🔟 Places to Eat

1 Restaurante Rancho de Chimayó
Authentic New Mexican cuisine, daily specials, and *sopaipillas* add to the charm of the historic adobe hacienda setting. ⊗ *Map D3 • CR 98 near Chimayó • 505-984-2100 • Closed Mon (Nov–mid-May) • Dis. access • $$*

2 Sugar Nymphs Bistro
Fresh ingredients and local produce enhance the creative American menu. Try the hand-tossed pizza or the signature chocolate maple pecan pie. ⊗ *Map E3 • 15046 NM 7b, Peñasco • 505-587-0311 • Open Nov–May: Wed–Sun; Closed Mon • $$*

3 Katherine's Restaurant
Freshly-prepared steaks, seafood, veal, shrimp, and pork draw a loyal clientele. ⊗ *Map D4 • 121 Longview Dr, White Rock • 505-672-9661 • Closed Mon & Sun • $$*

4 Chili Works
The lineups at this takeout spot start early, as locals, Los Alamos National Laboratory employees, and tourists gather for the hearty breakfast burrito. ⊗ *Map C4 • 1743 Trinity Dr, Los Alamos • 505-662-7591 • Closed Sun & Mon • $*

5 El Paragua Restaurant
Famed for its inspired New Mexican and American dishes, this place is bustling even on weeknights. The *sopaipillas* are served with homemade preserves. ⊗ *Map D3 • 603 Santa Cruz Rd, Espanola • 505-753-3211 • $$*

6 Embudo Station
Enjoy a glass of wine or beer, with a meal of country smoked ribs and trout, on the patio of this historic railroad station. ⊗ *Map D3 • NM 68, Embudo • 505-852-4707 • Closed Mon & Dec–early Apr • $$$*

7 Tesuque Village Market
This attractive café and market features indoor and patio seating, as well as classic and creative American and New Mexican fare. ⊗ *Map M1 • Bishop's Lodge Rd • 505-988-8848 • Partial dis. access • $$$*

8 Diego's Café
Stuffed *sopaipillas*, blue corn enchiladas, and margaritas are favorites at this popular local restaurant. Helpings are generous, and service is cheerful. ⊗ *Map G2 • 193 Paseo de Peralta • 505-983-5101 • Dis. access • $$*

9 Ruby K's Bagel Café
Fresh bagels and homemade breads are used for making creative hot, cold, and breakfast sandwiches. Good breakfast and lunch options. ⊗ *Map C4 • 1789 Central Ste 2, Los Alamos • 505-662-9866 • $*

10 Hill Diner
Legendary grilled chicken, burgers, steak, homemade soups, and Tex-Mex style chile are favorites at this American-style diner. Ribs served on Friday nights. ⊗ *Map C4 • 1315 Trinity Drive, Los Alamos • 505-662-9745 • $*

> *Unless otherwise stated, all restaurants are open daily, accept credit cards, and serve vegetarian dishes.*

Left **San Francisco de Asis** Center **Holy Cross Catholic Church** Right **Santuario de Chimayó**

🔟 The High Road to Taos

1 Holy Cross Catholic Church
Beautiful Spanish colonial religious artifacts are the centerpiece of this 1733 church. ✆ *Map D4 • Santa Cruz NM 76 • 505-753-3345 • Open daily, except noon–1pm*

2 Chimayó Museum
Located on one of the last remaining walled plazas in New Mexico, this 1995 museum offers a permanent exhibit of photographs and changing displays of local art. ✆ *Map D3 • Chimayó, NM 76 & NM 502 • 505-351-0945 • www.chimayomuseum.org*

3 Chimayó
Weaving traditions here have Spanish origins, but have developed over the past 300 years into the unique style known as Rio Grande. Several shops offer textiles. ✆ *Map D3*

4 Santuario de Chimayó
This beautiful chapel in Chimayó village attracts a surfeit of visitors each year. Many people are drawn by the legendary healing powers of the sacred earth found here *(see p75)*.

5 Cordova
Woodcarvers' community famed for the unpainted Cordova style of religious carving initiated by José Dolores López in the 1920s. ✆ *Map E3 • Just off of NM 76*

6 Truchas
Perched on a ridge beneath 13,100-ft (3,990-m) Truchas Peak, this mountain village was the backdrop for Robert Redford's film, *The Milagro Beanfield War (see p74)*.

7 Nuestra Señora del Sagrado Rosario Church
Also known as Our Lady of the Sacred Rosary, this adobe church has traditional religious carvings. ✆ *Map E3 • Truchas*

8 Las Trampas
The area's famed San José de Gracia Catholic Church is a fine example of early adobe church construction. ✆ *Map E3 • Church: open Jun–Aug 9am–5pm Mon–Sat*

9 Picuris Pueblo
Just out of Peñasco, is Picuris Pueblo, the smallest of New Mexico's pueblos. It is known for its clay pottery flecked with sparkling mica. ✆ *Map E3*

10 Church of San Francisco de Asis
One of New Mexico's most visited adobe churches is also one of the most photographed and painted sites *(see p72)*.

The High Road from Santa Fe to Taos passes through some stunning scenery.

Left & center **Bradbury Science Museum** Right **Soda Dam**

🔟 The Jémez Mountain Trail

1 White Rock Overlook
A short side-trip offers lovely views of the Sangre de Cristo Mountains and the Rio Grande River flowing through White Rock Canyon far below. ⬙ *Map D4 • Off NM 4 in White Rock • 505-672-3183*

2 Bandelier National Monument
The one-mile paved, self-guided Main Loop Trail in Frijoles Canyon leads past the striking village ruins and cliff dwellings of the Ancestral Pueblo peoples *(see pp30–31)*.

3 Bradbury Science Museum
More than 40 interactive exhibits highlight a range of science and technology projects at this Los Alamos Laboratory-operated museum *(see p72)*.

4 Valles Caldera National Preserve
The overlooks along the rim of this ancient volcano offer views down into and across the pastoral caldera dotted with forested volcanic domes *(see p74)*.

5 Jémez Falls
An easy one-mile round-trip hike, along a forested trail, offers views of the river as it drops 70 ft (21 m) in a series of waterfalls. ⬙ *Map C4 • 3 miles (5 km) off NM 4*

6 Battleship Rock
This towering rocky cliff rises above the river like the prow of a huge ship. Popular area for hiking and fishing. ⬙ *Map C4 • Along NM 4*

7 Soda Dam
A warm flow of water has draped the rocks with amazing mineral deposits, creating a natural dam blocking the Jémez River. ⬙ *Map C4 • Along NM 4*

8 Jémez State Monument
Visit stone ruins and a 17th-century Catholic mission church, San José de los Jémez, in the village of Giusewa. ⬙ *Map C4 • NM 4, Jémez Springs • 505-829-3530*

9 Jémez Springs
Natural hot springs amid scenic Jémez Mountains. The Jémez Springs Bathhouse offers mineral baths, massage, and spa treatments. ⬙ *Map C4 • NM 4 • 505-829-3303 • Open daily • Adm • www.jemezspringsbathhouse.com*

10 Jémez Pueblo
The red rock valley of the Jémez River is home to the Jémez Pueblo. Visit the small museum, a crafts and pottery shop, and seasonal roadside stands selling traditional foods and crafts. ⬙ *Map B4 • 7413 NM 4 • 505-834-7235 • www.jemezpueblo.org*

Two marked trails into the Valles Caldera National Preserve are open for day hikes without advance reservation.

79

Left & center **Museum of Indian Arts and Culture** Right **El Rancho de las Golondrinas**

Santa Fe South

HREE OF THE COUNTRY'S NATIONAL SCENIC BYWAYS *lead out of Santa Fe, following ancient paths used by Native Americans. Today, scenic backroads follow what was once El Camino Real south through Albuquerque, the route used by the Spanish colonial traders. To the east, I-25 follows the original Santa Fe Trail toward Pecos National Historical Park, where ruts carved in the rock by loaded wagons can still be seen. The Turquoise Trail runs through the Ortiz Mountains where Native Americans mined for turquoise. In the 1800s, the prospectors built shanty towns in the search for gold, silver, turquoise, lead, and finally, coal. These routes offer museums, historic sites, National Monuments and Parks, and artistic towns.*

🔟 Sights

1. Museum of International Folk Art
2. Museum of Indian Arts and Culture
3. The Museum of Spanish Colonial Art
4. El Rancho de las Golondrinas
5. Kasha-Katuwe Tent Rocks National Monument
6. Tinkertown Museum
7. Coronado State Monument
8. Pecos National Historical Park
9. Cerrillos
10. Madrid, Mine Shaft Tavern, and Museum

The Kasha-Katuwe Tent Rocks trail

Around Town – Santa Fe South

1 Museum of International Folk Art

Florence Bartlett (1881–1954), founder of the museum, selected Santa Fe for the museum's location based on its reputation for "mingling of cultures." The museum opened in 1953 with her collection of art from 37 countries. In 1982, the Girard Wing opened with displays selected from 100,000 objects given to the museum by folk art collector Alexander Girard. ✪ *Map L3 • 706 Camino Lejo • 505-476-1200 • Open 10am–5pm Tue–Sun • Adm • www.moifa.org*

Museum of International Folk Art

2 Museum of Indian Arts and Culture

With 80,000 cataloged items and more than 10 million artifacts, this 1987 museum boasts the most comprehensive collection of Native American anthropological articles in the country. Permanent exhibits showcase artifacts from regional pueblos, while changing exhibits present a broad range of subjects, from prehistoric tribal cultures to contemporary Native American art and sculpture.
✪ *Map L3 • 710 Camino Lejo • 505-476-1250 • Open 10am–5pm Tue–Sun • Adm • www.miaclab.org*

3 The Museum of Spanish Colonial Art

One of the world's most extensive collections of Spanish Colonial art is housed in this lovely John Gaw Meem-designed building. More than 3,000 objects trace the evolution of the Spanish Colonial arts traditions. The New Mexico collection features a wide range of religious and everyday artifacts used by the earliest Spanish settlers in New Mexico.
✪ *Map L3 • 750 Camino Lejo • 505-982-2226 • Open 10am–5pm daily • Adm • Dis. access • www.spanishcolonial.org*

4 El Rancho de las Golondrinas

Colonial life on a Spanish hacienda along the El Camino Real trade route is re-enacted in this exceptional living history museum. Many of the buildings are original to the site, and others have been moved on to the ranch from locations nearby. Structures essential to a self-sustaining Spanish hacienda are all here. The original Baca family adobe home with its defensive towers was built in the 1700s. The 1830s House of Manuel Baca features the out-buildings required to operate a ranch and vineyard *(see pp28–9)*.

5 Kasha-Katuwe Tent Rocks National Monument

The park derives its name from the massive tent-like conical formations created by wind and water erosion. The 3-mile (4.8-km) round-trip main trail leads through a narrow box canyon, with naturally-sculpted steep walls, and past the fascinating tent-shaped rocks. Farther along, the trail becomes steep and rough as it climbs to the mesa rim, where overlooks offer fabulous views of the valley. ✪ *Map C4 • W of Santa Fe • 505-761-8768 • Open summer: 7am–7pm; winter: 8am–5pm daily • $5 per vehicle*

There are no facilities or food at the Tent Rocks National Monument, so bring plenty of water and snacks with you.

→

Art Towns

The towns along the Turquoise Trail – Golden, Madrid, and Cerrillos – were quickly abandoned when the mining ended. The clapboard buildings that housed miners remained empty until the 1970s, when artists began moving in. Today, Madrid and Cerrillos are established artistic towns with numerous shops and galleries.

6 Tinkertown Museum

Ross Ward (1941–2002) hand-carved, painted, collected, and conceived every part of these delightful exhibits. He traveled widely, collecting antiques, toys, and interesting bits-and-pieces discarded by others. The result is 22 amazing rooms filled with American folk art. Many of the displays are mechanical, creating an entire Wild Western town that comes to life as animated characters visit the dentist, interact on the street, and shop in the general store. ◈ Map C6 • 121 Sandia Crest Rd, Sandia Park • 505-281-5233 • Open Apr–Oct 9am–6pm daily • Adm

7 Coronado State Monument

Some of the finest examples of Pre-Columbian mural art in North America are displayed here. The colorful murals, depicting planting and harvest scenes, were discovered in the 1930s during the excavation of Kuaua Pueblo, which was built about 1325. A short path leads to numerous ruins, including a partially reconstructed ceremonial kiva where the murals were found. Several of the preserved murals are on display in the Visitors' Center, which also has exhibits of Native and Spanish Colonial artifacts. ◈ Map C5 • 485 Kuaua Rd, off NM 44/US 550, Bernalillo • 505-867-5351 • Open 8:30am–5pm Wed–Mon • Dis. access • www.nmmonuments.org

8 Pecos National Historical Park

In the 1800s, the remains of Pecos Pueblo were the last major landmark seen by travelers on the Santa Fe Trail before reaching Santa Fe. Today, the ruins reveal the area's history, with displays relating to Pecos Pueblo, the Santa Fe Trail, and the American Civil War Battle of Glorieta Pass. Ranger guided tours can be scheduled to see Santa Fe Trail sites, an old stage depot, and the site of the Battle of Glorieta Pass. ◈ Map E5 • Hwy 63, off I-25 at exit 307, Pecos • 505-757-6414 • Open summer: 8am–6pm daily; winter: 8am–5pm daily • Dis. access • www.nps.gov/peco

9 Cerrillos

The Ortiz Mountains surrounding Cerrillos were formed with an abundance of mineral deposits. Before the Pueblo Revolt of 1680, the Spanish forced Pueblo Indians to work in

An attractive mural in the Coronado State Monument

A view of present-day Cerrillos

silver mines here. The modern era of mining began when gold was discovered in 1879. Soon, deposits of silver, copper, lead, zinc, and turquoise were found, and the heyday of mining for precious metals had arrived. It all ended quickly, making way for coal mining in Madrid as the economic mainstay. Today, Cerrillos is a sleepy town with many attractive false-front buildings, a charming church, and traditional adobe buildings on the backstreets. ◈ Map D5

10 Madrid, Mine Shaft Tavern, and Museum

Madrid was built as a company town in the 1800s. With shafts as deep as 2,500 ft (762 m), it was one of the world's rare areas that mined both hard and soft coal. The town thrived for a time, becoming known for its Christmas celebration and Fourth of July parade. In 1959, Los Alamos, the mine's last customer, switched to electricity and Madrid quickly became a ghost town. Much of the equipment remained and the mine site has been re-opened as a museum. The original company tavern is still open. The current residents have revived many of the former mining-town holiday celebrations. The Madrid Blues Festival is held on several summer Sundays. ◈ Map D5

Museum Highlights Drive

Morning

Have breakfast at funky **Harry's Roadhouse** (see p85). Drive to **El Rancho de las Golondrinas** (see pp28–9), by going south on I-25 to exit 276 and bear right on NM 599. Turn left at the traffic light on to Frontage Road and turn right just before the race track on Los Pinos Road. Turn left into El Rancho de las Golondrinas and explore the historic Spanish Colonial living-history museum. Return to I-25 via the ramp and drive north to exit 284, the Old Pecos Trail, and then head north toward Santa Fe Plaza. Turn right on Old Santa Fe Trail and right again at Camino Lejo. Continue to **Museum Hill** (see pp16–17). Park near the **International Museum of Folk Art** (see p81). Take the stairs up to **Milner Plaza** (see p16) for views of the Sangre de Cristo Mountains. Enjoy a meal at the Museum Hill Café (see p16).

Afternoon:

Walk over to the **Museum of Indian Arts and Culture** (see p81) and stroll through the **Here, Now and Always** (see p16) exhibit. Take your time to see the rest of the museum. Then head over to the International Folk Art Museum and leisurely explore the colorful folk art at the **Girard Wing**. Don't miss the latest exhibit in the **Neutrogena Wing**. Visit **The Museum of Spanish Colonial Art** (see p81) next door. The museum is housed in a John Gaw Meem-designed adobe residence and the unique Spanish Colonial artworks can be seen in less than an hour.

Left **An old truck at the Old Coal Mine Museum** Center **Madrid** Right **Casa Grande Trading Post**

TOP 10 The Turquoise Trail

1 Cerrillos Hills Historic Park
Several miles of hiking and mountain biking trails that lead through the mining district. ◈ *Map D5 • NM 14, N of Cerrillos*

2 Casa Grande Trading Post and Mining Museum
This museum is packed with early mining exhibits and artifacts. The owners have a local hard-rock mine that produces turquoise. ◈ *Map D5 • 17 Waldo, Cerrillos • 505-438-3008 • Open 8am–sunset • Adm*

3 Cerrillos
A picturesque town with a flavor of the Wild West that made it perfect for the movie *All the Pretty Horses (see p82).*

4 Old Coal Mine Museum and Engine House Theatre
Examine the remains of the Madrid coal mine. A former locomotive repair building, now a theater, presents plays in the summer. ◈ *Map D5 • 2846 NM 14 • 505-438-3780 • Open 9:30am–5pm Mon–Fri, summer; 9:30am–6pm Sat & Sun; winter: 10am–4pm Sat & Sun • Adm*

5 Madrid
Madrid became a ghost town in the 1950s when the mines closed. Revived in the 1970s, it is today an eclectic village of galleries and shops *(see p83).*

6 Golden
This village appeared when gold deposits were discovered in the 1840s. The gold soon ran out, and by the 1880s, Golden was abandoned. Don't miss the lovely adobe church. ◈ *Map D5*

7 Museum of Archaeology and Material Culture
The region's history is presented through exhibits of prehistoric Native American artifacts. ◈ *Map C6 • 22 Calvary Rd, Cedar Crest, off NM 14 • 505-281-4745 • Open May–Oct noon–7pm • Adm*

8 Tinkertown Museum
Painted miniature figures in tiny "towns" animate at the push of a button *(see p82).*

9 Sandia Crest National Scenic Byway
Spectacular vistas enroute through the Cibola National Forest to Sandia Crest. ◈ *Map C6 • NM 536*

10 Sandia Peak
A pretty mountain, dominating the Albuquerque skyline. In summer, Sandia Peak Ski Area offers a ski lift to the summit and trailheads for serious hiking. ◈ *Map C6 • Sandia Ski Area • 505-242-9052 • Ski lift: Open 10am–4pm Fri–Sun • Adm*

The Turquoise Trail is 70 miles (113 km) of the scenic road that weaves through small towns surrounded by piñon-covered mountains.

Price Categories

For a three-course meal for one, with half a bottle of wine (or equivalent meal), including taxes and extra charges.

$	under $20
$$	$20–40
$$$	$40–55
$$$$	$55–80
$$$$$	over $80

Above **Mine Shaft Tavern**

🔟 Places to Eat

1 Harry's Roadhouse
The extensive menu includes the favorite American and New Mexican comfort foods done to perfection. Daily specials add an adventurous touch, such as whole-wheat fettuccini with braised duck. ◎ *Map D4 • 96B Old Las Vegas Hwy • 505-989-4629 • $$*

2 Mine Shaft Tavern
Historic tavern, with a long stand-up bar and murals by Ross Ward. The menu features burgers, smoked chicken, steaks, burritos, and enchiladas. ◎ *Map D5 • 2846 NM 14, Madrid • 505-473-0743 • $$*

3 PAA-KO Ridge Golf Club
Ideal for a simple lunch of soup, salad, and sandwiches on the patio with views of the Sandia Mountains. ◎ *Map D6 • 1 Club House Dr, Sandia Park NM 14 Turquoise Trail • 505-281-6000 • $*

4 San Marcos Cafe
Charming country café, with a delectable breakfast and lunch menu featuring Continental and New Mexican cuisine. ◎ *Map D5 • 3877 NM 14, San Marcos, Turquoise Trail • 505-471-9298 • Partial dis. access • $$*

5 Java Junction Coffee
A favorite local gathering place for coffee and lunch. Sandwiches, pastries, and a full complement of coffees, including latte, espresso, and cappuccino. ◎ *Map D5 • 2855 NM 14, Turquoise Trail, Madrid • 505-438-2772 • $*

6 Chocolate Maven
Legendary desserts and gourmet sandwiches. Saturday and Sunday brunch are exceptionally popular. Look through the windows into the kitchen as the bakers create their masterpieces. High tea served 3–5pm, Mon–Fri. ◎ *Map L2 • 821 W San Mateo Rd, Santa Fe • 505-984-1980 • $*

7 Counter Culture
This trendy, order-at-the-counter joint offers irresistible soups, salads, and sandwiches. No credit cards accepted. ◎ *Map L2 • 930 Baca St, Santa Fe • 505-995-1105 • Open evenings • Dis. access • $$*

8 Cloud Cliff Bakery
Enjoy a breakfast or a lunch featuring organic, locally grown food, fresh baked breads, and desserts. Try the fish tacos with baby spinach. ◎ *Map L2 • 1805 2nd St, Santa Fe • 505-983-6254 • $$*

9 Dara Thai
Authentic Thai food is served at this casual family owned diner. Try the Tom Ga Gai, a chicken soup with herbs and lemongrass in a coconut milk broth. ◎ *Map L2 • 1710 Cerrillos Rd, Santa Fe • 505-995-0887 • Closed Sun • $$*

10 Range Café at Bernalillo
Western-style restaurant with cowboy hats and art on the walls. American and New Mexican favorites include enchiladas and burritos. ◎ *Map C5 • 925 Camino del Pueblo, Bernalillo • 505-867-1700 • $$*

Unless otherwise stated, all restaurants are open daily, accept credit cards, and serve vegetarian dishes.

Left & center **Kit Carson Home and Museum** Right **Millicent Rogers Museum**

Taos Area

RISING ABOVE THE TAOS PLAIN, *Taos Mountain has long been sacred to the Pueblo Indians who settled near its base. The pueblo they built here is one of the oldest continually occupied villages in North America. In 1992, it became a UNESCO World Heritage Site. The dramatic landscapes, warm light, and high desert air have drawn artists to this region, and their galleries and studios have created a bustling artists' hub. Hordes of outdoor enthusiasts come here to hike and bike the spectacular mountain and desert trails, fish sparkling streams, raft on the raging whitewater of the Rio Grande, and test themselves on the slopes of one of America's finest ski resorts.*

🔟 Sights

1. Taos Old Town
2. Taos Pueblo
3. Rancho de Taos
4. Taos Ski Valley
5. Taos Art Museum at the Fechin House
6. The Harwood Museum of Art
7. Rio Grande Gorge Bridge
8. Millicent Rogers Museum
9. Kit Carson Home and Museum
10. E.L. Blumenschein Home and Museum

Colorful façade of an art gallery in Taos

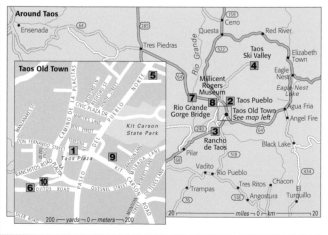

Preceding pages: **Taos Ski Valley**

Pillared portals, Taos Old Town

Taos Old Town
Easy to explore on foot, this quirky town offers numerous art galleries, some of which rival those in Santa Fe for quality and price, and others that present the works of emerging and local artists at affordable prices. Other shops, particularly the Bent Street outlets, offer unique handicrafts *(see pp20–21)*.

Taos Pueblo
One of the few Native American groups that have never been conquered or displaced, the Taos Pueblo Indians have lived at the foot of Taos Mountain for more than a millennium. The pueblo complex that they built has changed little in the past 600 years, and its elegant lines have inspired artists for decades. The pueblo is open to visitors daily, except when sacred ceremonies are taking place *(see pp22–3)*.

Rancho de Taos
Settled by the Spanish in 1716, this village is best known for the famous San Francisco de Asis Church *(see p73)*. The church is surrounded by remodeled adobe buildings containing shops, galleries, and restaurants. Nearby, La Hacienda de los Martinez was once a stop along the El Camino Real trade route. Restored period rooms,

exhibits, and demonstrations of weaving and blacksmithing illustrate Spanish colonial life on the frontier. ⊗ *Map E2 • La Hacienda de los Martinez: 708 Hacienda Rd • 575-758-1000 • Open Apr–Oct 10am–5pm Mon–Sat, noon–5pm Sun, Nov–Mar 10am–4pm daily • Adm*

Taos Ski Valley
With over 300 inches (762 cm) of snow each year and one of the nation's steepest slopes, Taos Ski Valley is one of the most popular ski resorts in the country. Set in a beautiful mountain valley, the resort offers beginner, intermediate, and expert runs. There are serious hiking trails leading to Wheeler Peak (16 miles roundtrip) and Williams Lake (8 miles roundtrip). ⊗ *Map E2 • 575-776-2233 • www.taosskivalley.com*

Taos Art Museum at the Fechin House
Internationally renowned, Russian-born artist Nicolai Fechin moved to Taos in 1927. He remodeled this beautiful adobe home, adding Russian-style woodcarvings into the staircase, doors, mantles, and cupboards. Besides showcasing Fechin's personal art collection and carved furniture, the home serves as the gallery for the Taos Art Museum. ⊗ *Map Q2 • 227 Paseo del Pueblo Norte • 575-758-2690 • Open 10am–5pm Tue–Sun • Partial dis. access • Adm • www.taosartmuseum.org*

Horno at Rancho de Taos

A spectacular view of the Rio Grande Gorge Bridge

Trading Center

Far away from Spanish control based in Santa Fe, Taos became a trading center in the 1700s. Every fall, a truce occurred, allowing trade between Native American tribes, and later, Spanish settlers and Anglos. After Mexican Independence in 1821, American trappers, including Kit Carson and Charles Bent, came here to trade their furs.

The Harwood Museum of Art

A favorite of Taos residents, this small museum was founded by Elizabeth Harwood in 1923 in memory of her husband, artist Burt Harwood. Works by artists with connections to Taos, including several by members of the celebrated Taos Society of Artists, are featured here. The museum's outstanding Hispanic collection includes 18th and 19th century religious artifacts, decorative tinwork, furniture, and the largest public collection of carvings by Patrociño Barela.
Map N3 • 238 Ledoux St • 575-758-9826 • Open 10am–5pm Tue–Sat, noon–5pm Sun • Dis. access • Adm • www.harwoodmuseum.org

Rio Grande Gorge Bridge

The view from the middle of the second-highest suspension bridge in the country is stunning. A walkway leads halfway across the 500-ft (152-m) span to an observation deck that offers an excellent place to gaze 650 ft (198 m) down into the gorge at the river rapids below. There are no fences at the top of the canyon, so exercise caution.
Map E2 • US 64, 12 miles (19 km) W of Taos

Millicent Rogers Museum

Oil heiress and fashion designer Millicent Rogers created a popular fashion style by synthesizing elements of Native American clothing with her natural flamboyance. Exhibits include her Southwest-inspired jewelry collection, the Maria Martinez (see p39) family collection of pottery, and a wide variety of Navajo, Pueblo, Hopi, and Zuni works. Other displays include Hispanic religious and secular art, Rio Grande weavings, and Hispanic tools. Map E2 • 1504 Millicent Rogers Rd • 575-758-2462 • Open Apr–Oct 10am–5pm daily, Nov–Mar closed Mon • Dis. access • Adm • www.millicentrogers.com

Jewelry, Millicent Rogers Museum

There are no fences at the top of the Rio Grande Gorge Bridge canyon, so stay on the trail and exercise caution.

Interior of Kit Carson Home and Museum

9 Kit Carson Home and Museum

Kit Carson, legendary scout and Western hero, purchased this adobe home for his bride, Josefa Jaramillo, in 1843. The house is a living history museum with costumed interpreters who tell the story of his life. ⊛ Map P2 • 113 Kit Carson Rd • 575-758-4945 • Open 9am–6pm daily (call for winter hours) • Dis. access • Adm • www.kitcarsonhome.com

10 E.L. Blumenschein Home and Museum

Instrumental in forming the Taos Society of Artists, Ernest Blumenschein first visited the Southwest in 1896 to do a series of illustrations for the *McClures* magazine. In 1919, he moved to Taos and lived in this house with his family. The home, furnishings, family possessions, and art collection on display are much the same as when the Blumenschein family lived here. Paintings by early Taos artists, and a blend of fine European furnishings and Spanish Colonial antiques are also housed here. ⊛ Map N3 • 222 Ledoux St • 575-758-0505 • Open May–Oct 9am–5pm daily (call for winter hours) • Adm • www.taoshistoricmuseums.com

Taos Pueblo and Taos by Car

Morning

🕐 Arrive at **Taos Pueblo** *(see pp22–3)* by mid-morning to see this ancient village before the crowds arrive. After an hour or so drive south and take Paseo del Pueblo Norte into Taos. Park near **Michael's Kitchen** *(see p93)*, but before having lunch, go across the street to enjoy the **Taos Art Museum at the Fechin House** *(see p89)*. Fechin's house, with hand-carved woodwork, is as interesting a piece of art as the art hung on the walls. Then walk back across the street to join the fast-moving line of people waiting to lunch at Michael's Kitchen.

Afternoon

Drive farther south on Paseo del Pueblo Norte and park near the corner of Kit Carson Road. Walk over to the **Kit Carson Home and Museum** and learn about the life of America's famous mountain man. For the rest of the afternoon enjoy the galleries located nearby. Turn left as you leave the Kit Carson Museum and visit **Wilder Nightingale Fine Art** *(see p92)*. Across the street from the Kit Carson Museum is **Total Arts Gallery** *(see p92)*. Around the corner on Paseo del Pueblo Norte is **The Taos Gallery** *(see p92)*. When you have seen the galleries, walk west to **Taos Plaza** *(see pp20–21)* and browse the antiques at **Maison Faurie** *(see p47)* then visit **Hotel La Fonda de Taos** *(see p21)* to see D.H. Lawrence's forbidden art. Stop in one of the hotel shops for ice cream or a cup of coffee. For a more formal atmosphere, check out the fine dining restaurants.

Above **Parks Gallery**

TOP 10 Art Galleries

1 The Taos Gallery
Creative arrangements of sculptures and paintings make for an attractive gallery. ✪ *Map P2 • 103 Paseo del Pueblo Norte • 575-758-3911 • www.terriebennettgallerie.com*

2 Total Arts Gallery, Inc
Exhibits include Impressionist works, abstracts, and contemporary realism. ✪ *Map P2 • 122-A Kit Carson Rd • 575-758-4667 • www.totalartsgallery.com*

3 Mission Gallery
Early Taos works of art and handmade prints are displayed in the former home of painter Joseph Henry Sharp. ✪ *Map P3 • 138 Kit Carson Rd • 575-758-2861*

4 Nichols Taos Fine Art Gallery
Oil and watercolor paintings, pastels, pencil and charcoal drawings are on display. ✪ *Map Q1 • 403 Paseo del Pueblo Norte • 575-758-2475 • www.nicholsgallery.com*

5 Wilder Nightingale Fine Art
Taos-style paintings, depicting the rich forms and bold colors of the Southwest are exhibited in this contemporary gallery. ✪ *Map P2 • 119 Kit Carson Rd • 575-758-3255 • www.wnightingale.com*

6 Parks Gallery
The paintings, sculptures, and prints by a handful of modern artists are often bold, dramatic, or abstract. ✪ *Map P2 • 127 Bent Street • 575-751-0343 • www.parksgallery.com*

7 Six Directions
A gallery of Southwestern arts and crafts located on the historic plaza. Highlights include hand crafted Navajo jewelry ✪ *Map P2 • 129B North Plaza • 575-758-5844 • www.sixdirect.com*

8 Lumina
A three-acre sculpture garden with the Sangre de Cristo Mountains as backdrop and tall stainless steel spires. ✪ *Map E2 • NM 230 Arroyo Seco • 575-776-0123 • www.luminagallery.com*

9 Brazos Fine Art
Dramatic art by nationally acclaimed Southwestern artists, along with glass and bronze works. ✪ *Map P2 • 119 Bent St • 575-758-0767 • www.brazosgallery.com*

10 Robert L. Parsons Fine Art
Works by early Taos artists as well as 19th-century Navajo weavings and Pueblo pottery. ✪ *Map P2 • 131 Bent St • 575-751-0159 • www.parsonsart.com*

Art galleries are usually open daily, though some may be closed on Mondays, weekends, or holidays. Call for timings.

Price Categories

For a three-course meal	**$** under $20
for one, with half a bottle	**$$** $20–40
of wine (or equivalent	**$$$** $40–55
meal), including taxes	**$$$$** $55–80
and extra charges.	**$$$$$** over $80

Above **Joseph's Table**

🔟 Places to Eat

1 The Stakeout
American steak and seafood restaurant, serving organic New York strip steaks, lamb chops, sea bass, and pasta. Panoramic mountain views from the patio. Extensive wine list. ✆ *Map E2 • 101 Stakeout Dr • 575-758-2042 • $$$$*

2 Michael's Kitchen
Popular for hearty helpings of comfort food, including American and New Mexican favorites. Irresistible fresh baked goods. ✆ *Map Q1 • 304 Paseo del Pueblo Norte • 575-758-4178 • $$*

3 Bent Street Café & Deli
This delightful country-style café is the perfect place to linger over a traditional breakfast. Try their creative sandwiches. ✆ *Map P2 • 120 Bent St • 575-758-5787 • $$*

4 The Bean
The best coffee and lattes in town. Coffee is roasted in the kitchen, and the pastries are freshly made. Limited menu, with daily specials. The selection ranges from breakfast burritos to burgers, veggie wraps, and shrimp tacos. ✆ *Map E2 • 1033 Paseo del Pueblo Sur • 575-758-5123 • $*

5 Doc Martin's
Legendary Taos gathering spot. The award-winning cuisine is contemporary American with New Mexican influences. Fabulous wine list and an adobe patio bar. ✆ *Map P2 • 125 Paseo del Pueblo Norte • 575-758-1977 • $$$*

6 Tim's Stray Dog Cantina
In the center of Taos Ski Valley, this chalet-style spot serves New Mexican and American food and evening wine and cocktails. ✆ *Map E2 • 105 Sutton Pl • 575-776-2894 • $$*

7 Joseph's Table
Nationally recognized for fine Continental dining in a historic location. The braised lamb shank with apple mint glaze can be enhanced with an exceptional wine list. ✆ *Map P2 • 108-A S Taos Plaza • 575-751-4512 • Partial dis. access • $$$$*

8 Texas Red's Steakhouse
This bright Wild West-style saloon and restaurant serves juicy steaks, as well as burgers, trout, and shrimp. ✆ *Map F1 • E Main St, Red River • 575-754-2922 • $$*

9 The Roasted Clove
Elegant fine dining, featuring entrées of filet mignon, ultra fresh tuna, elk, and succulent pork tenderloin. The desserts are decadent. ✆ *Map F2 • 48 North Angel Fire Rd, Angel Fire • 575-377-0636 • $$*

10 Café Abiquiu
In the heart of Georgia O'Keeffe country, this pretty country café offers an assortment of creative entrées. An exceptional on-site giftshop stocks an extensive collection of O'Keeffe-related books, calendars, and prints. ✆ *Map C3 • US 84, Abiquiu • 575-685-4378 • $$*

Left **Wild Rivers Recreation Area** Right **D.H. Lawrence Memorial**

ⓉⓄⓅ10 The Enchanted Circle

1 D.H. Lawrence Memorial

The famous author completed his novella *St. Mawr* here, during 1924–25. The memorial can be visited, but the ranch buildings are closed to the public. ◈ *Map E2* • *NM 522, N of US 64* • *575-776-2245*

2 Questa

This lovely lakeside village is known for St. Anthony's Church, where religious artworks by local craftspeople are housed. ◈ *Map E1* • *Visitors' Center, Questa* • *575-586-0443*

3 Wild Rivers Recreation Area

Scenic views of the gorges from 800 ft (244 m) above the Rio Grande and the Red River. ◈ *Map E2* • *NM 522, Cerro* • *575-758-8851*

4 Red River

This former miners' boom-town today boasts a funky Wild West ambience. In winter, it is a family-friendly ski resort. ◈ *Map F1* • *Red River Visitor Center: 575-754-3030* • *Red River Ski Area: 575-754-2223*

5 Bobcat Pass

The road from Red River to Eagle Nest offers spectacular views of green alpine valleys amid towering peaks of the Sangre de Cristo Mountains. ◈ *Map F2*

6 Eagle Nest

Much less touristy than Red River, the Eagle Nest Lake State Park is a favorite year-round destination for trout and salmon fishermen. ◈ *Map F2* • *800-494-9117*

7 Cimarron Canyon State Park

The dramatic Cimarron Canyon is a favorite with hikers, campers, and fly fishermen. The sheer rock walls of Cimarron Palisades are spectacular. ◈ *Map F2* • *575-377-6271*

8 Vietnam Veterans Memorial State Park

The nation's first monument honoring Vietnam veterans was built in honor of David Westphall by his family. ◈ *Map F2* • *US 64, NE of Angel Fire* • *575-377-6900* • *Open 9am–5pm daily* • *Donation*

9 Angel Fire

Perennial recreation features skiing in winter; hiking, mountain biking, and fishing in summer. ◈ *Map F2* • *Angel Fire information, 800-633-7463* • *Angel Fire Resort, 575-377-6401, www.angelfireresort.com*

10 Taos Canyon

The road from Angel Fire to Taos follows this narrow, forested canyon as it winds through the mountains. In the lower canyon several artists' studios are open to the public. ◈ *Map E2*

This spectacular 84-mile (135-km) scenic route circles 13,160-ft (4,010-m) Wheeler Mountain, New Mexico's highest.

Above **A spectacular view of the Earthships community**

 # Rio Grande & O'Keeffe Country

1 Millicent Rogers Museum
This exceptional collection features beautiful Southwestern, Native American, and Hispanic art, much of which was in Rogers' personal collection (*see p90*).

2 Rio Grande Gorge Bridge
America's second-highest suspension bridge spans 500 ft (152 m) across the gorge. An observation deck on the bridge provides an incredible view down the river gorge (*see p90*).

3 Earthships
This environmental community features homes with self-sustaining energy systems. Daily tours of a model home include viewing an informative video. ✆ *Map E2 • US 64 • 575-751-0462 • Open 10am–4pm daily • Adm*

4 Hopewell Lake Recreation Area
Surrounded by the aspen-forested San Juan Mountains, this lovely alpine lake has brook and rainbow trout for fishing. ✆ *Map C2 • US 64*

5 Brazos Cliffs
The 11,400-ft (3,475-m) sheer rock Brazos Cliffs are composed of Precambrian quartzite, some of the oldest rock in New Mexico. ✆ *Map C2 • US 64 overlook*

6 Echo Amphitheater
This natural amphitheater offers a picnic area, a campground, and short walking trails. ✆ *Map C2 • US 84 • 575-684-2486*

7 Ghost Ranch
Today, the ranch is owned by the Presbyterian church and offers an extensive selection of workshops, primarily in the arts and crafts. ✆ *Map C2 • US 84, Abiquiu • 575-685-4333 • www. ghostranch.org*

8 Museums at Ghost Ranch
The Florence Hawley Ellis Museum of Anthropology and the Ruth Hall Museum of Paleontology present ancient Pueblo pottery and dinosaur fossils found on the ranch. ✆ *Map C2 • US 84, Abiquiu • 575-685-4333 • www.ghostranch.org*

9 Abiquiu
Frequently painted by Georgia O'Keeffe, today this town and valley are home to organic farmers and artists. ✆ *Map C3*

10 Georgia O'Keeffe House and Studio Tour
Make reservations months in advance (unless you get lucky with a cancellation) if you want to tour the famous artist's home. ✆ *Map C3 • Abiquiu • 505-685-4539 • Tours by appt only: Mar–Nov Tue, Thu, & Fri • Adm*

Above **Anderson-Abruzzo International Balloon Museum**

Albuquerque Area

NEW MEXICO'S LARGEST CITY, *Albuquerque is one of the fastest growing urban areas in the Southwest. The economy is diverse, successfully blending education, arts, finance, and high-tech to create a modern multicultural city. Albuquerque is noted for its outstanding symphony orchestra, contemporary museums, airport, and an eclectic mix of artists, musicians, filmmakers, and writers. Founded in 1706, the city began as a humble Spanish farming village in the area now known as Old Town. Route 66, America's "Mother Road", opened in 1926, and Albuquerque expanded along the ribbon of highway.*

TOP 10 Sights

1. Petroglyph National Monument
2. San Felipe de Neri Catholic Church
3. Albuquerque Museum of Art and History
4. New Mexico Museum of Natural History and Science
5. Sandia Peak Tramway
6. Anderson-Abruzzo International Balloon Museum
7. Albuquerque BioPark/ Aquarium and Rio Grande Botanic Gardens
8. Indian Pueblo Cultural Center
9. Turquoise Museum
10. Rio Grande Zoo

Street Mural in Albuquerque

1 Petroglyph National Monument

An estimated 25,000 ancient petroglyphs were carved into the black volcanic rocks centuries ago, by the ancestors of the Pueblo Indians and, more recently, by the early Spanish settlers. Many of the images are of animals, people, and symbols, while others are more complex and difficult to identify. Several short self guiding trails lead to hundreds of petroglyphs.
🗺 *Map B6 • Visitors' Center, 4735 Unser Blvd • 505-899-0205 • Open 8am–5pm daily • Adm • www.nps.gov/petr*

2 San Felipe de Neri Catholic Church

Originally founded by the Franciscans in 1706, the church was given a new roof, altar, and pulpit on orders from Bishop Lamy in 1853. The overhaul continued when Lamy invited Jesuit priests from Italy to oversee a major renovation of the church and the adjacent buildings, adding a European flair. Today, this lovely church draws visitors to tour its cool interior, while the Parish museum displays furnishings and religious art once used in the church. 🗺 *Map P5 • 2005 N Plaza NW• 505-243-4628 • Open 8am–5pm daily*

3 Albuquerque Museum of Art and History

This nationally recognized museum completed a major expansion in 2004, adding a huge new gallery to host world-class traveling exhibits. The Taos Society of Artists paintings are exceptional, and the museum's art collection has numerous outstanding historic and contemporary works by regional artists. The presentation of the

"Earth Mother", Albuquerque Museum of Art and History

history exhibits are a bit dated by current standards, but the Spanish Colonial collection is impressive, and is one of the largest in the country. Be sure to see the imposing life-size models of Spanish conquistadors dressed in full armor.
🗺 *Map P5 • 2000 Mountain Rd • 505-243-7255 • Open 9am–5pm Tue–Sun • Dis. access • Adm • www. cabq.gov/museum*

4 New Mexico Museum of Natural History and Science

Throughout this exceptionally well-planned and executed museum, interactive exhibits bring to life the geological and natural history of the Southwest. Starting with the formation of the universe, time-sequenced exhibits tell the story of New Mexico through the centuries, right up to the present with a Mars Lander on display. The Dyna Theater offers films on a five-story Extreme Screen with surround sound. 🗺 *Map P5 • 1801 Mountain Rd • 505-841-2800 • Open 9am–5pm daily, except Thanksgiving, Christmas, & non-holiday Mon in Jan & Sep • Dis. access • Adm • www.nmnaturalhistory.org*

The Visitors' Center provides a park brochure, information, and directions to the walking trail in Petroglyph National Monument.

Ballooning Firsts

Albuquerque's Balloon Fiesta has grown from 13 balloons in 1972 to more than 700 balloons in recent years. The first successful non-stop crossing of the Atlantic Ocean was made in 1978 by Ben Abruzzo, Maxie Anderson, and Larry Newman. In 1981, Abruzzo, Anderson, and two others became the first to cross the Pacific Ocean by helium balloon.

Façade, Anderson-Abruzzo International Balloon Museum

5 Sandia Peak Tramway

The world's longest aerial tramway takes sightseers, hikers, and skiers to the top of the Sandia Mountains year round. The summit offers panoramic views and there are food outlets both here and at the bottom of the tramway. On the ride up or down, watch for muledeer, black bear, and raccoons. ◈ *Map C6 • I-25, exit 234, Tramway Rd • 505-856-7325 • Open Memorial Day–Labor Day 9am–9pm daily, Labor Day–Memorial Day 9am–8pm daily (5pm–8pm Tue) • Adm • www.sandiapeak.com*

6 Anderson-Abruzzo International Balloon Museum

Interactive exhibits, ballooning artifacts, and first-person accounts present the history, art, science, and sport of ballooning. Some of the artifacts date to the earliest days of ballooning.

◈ *Map C6 • 9201 Balloon Museum Dr NE • 505-768-6020 • Open 9am–5pm Tue–Sun • Dis. access • Adm • www.cabq.gov/balloon*

7 Albuquerque BioPark/ Aquarium and Rio Grande Botanic Gardens

The dramatic highlight of the striking aquarium is the 285,000 gallon ocean tank where Gulf of Mexico brown, sandtiger, blacktip, and nurse sharks swim with brilliantly colored coral reef fish, sea turtles, and open ocean fish. Across the plaza, the Botanic Gardens provide a lush oasis bordering the Rio Grande River. The colorful Spanish-Moorish garden is one of three walled gardens. ◈ *Map C6 • 2601 Central Ave NW, Tingley Park • 505-764-6200 • Open 9am–5pm daily, Jul & Aug 9am–6pm Sat & Sun • Adm • www. cabq.gov/biopark*

8 Indian Pueblo Cultural Center

Owned and operated by the 19 pueblos of New Mexico, this museum presents Pueblo culture through a series of exhibits. Each pueblo displays its traditional crafts. Native American dances, bread-baking, and craft demonstrations are held every weekend. ◈ *Map C6 • 2401 12th St NW • 505-843-7270 • Open 9am–5pm daily • Dis. access • www.indianpueblo.org*

Courtyard, Indian Pueblo Cultural Center

During the annual Balloon Fiesta, the Sandia Peak Tramway offers extended hours, from 9am–9pm.

Turquoise Museum

9 This remarkable family-owned museum presents every aspect of the "sky stone" in fascinating and understandable displays. Discover what to ask when buying turquoise jewelry. A simulated mine shaft leads to fine examples of stones from mines around the world, and a lapidary area shows how turquoise is cut and polished. A superb collection of turquoise jewelry is for sale in the adjacent shop. ® *Map N5 • 2107 Central Ave NW • 505-247-8650 • Open 9:30am–4pm Mon–Fri, 9:30am–3pm Sat • Adm*

Exhibits at the Turquoise Museum

Rio Grande Zoo

10 This zoo is home to more than 250 species of exotic and native animals who reside in naturalistic habitats with trees, grass, water features, and rockwork. Exceptional exhibits include the rare snow leopard. The mountain lion catwalk lets the caged cats walk over the pedestrian path. The giraffes and Asian elephants, a pride of lions, and the red kangaroo are also popular. The polar bears can be viewed swimming underwater, and the seals and sea lions are fed at 10:30am and 3:30pm daily. In the summer, there is a children's petting zoo and a Zoo Music concert series most Friday evenings. ® *Map C6 • 903 10th St SW • 505-764-6200 • Open 9am–5pm daily • Closed major hols • Dis. access • Adm*

A Walk Around Old Town

Morning

🕐 Start at the **Albuquerque Museum of Art and History** *(see pp97)* and allow about two hours to see the exhibits and explore the history of Albuquerque and New Mexico. Exit the museum and walk through the parking lot to enter the pedestrian pathway under the arch. This shop-lined walk emerges into **Old Town** *(see pp26–7)* near the **Plaza** *(see p26)*. Enter **San Felipe de Neri Church** *(see p97)* across from the Plaza. Before leaving, see the small museum. When you exit, walk around the block to Church Street. Have lunch or a snack at **Church Street Café** *(see p101)*, in the middle of the block.

Afternoon

Turn right on Church Street to the corner of Romero, and right again to the specialty shop **Hispaniae** *(see p100)* selling New Mexican folk art. Turn left and stroll to 320 Romero, which houses **Trader Barbs Gallery** of Native American jewelry. Across the street in Plazuela Sombra, visit the **R.C. Gorman/Nizhoni Gallery**. Continue down Romero to Plaza Don Luis to the **Weems Gallery** *(see p100)*. Continue on Romero to South Plaza Street and turn right. Walk one block to Rio Grande Boulevard and cross over to the strip mall facing **Route 66 and Central Avenue** *(see p27)* and visit the must-see **Turquoise Museum**. Return to Romero and turn left. Walk north to **Crave Ice Cream & Coffee** for a treat.

Left **Weems Gallery Old Town** Center **Hispaniae** Right **Mariposa Gallery**

🔟 Galleries and Shops

Around Town – Albuquerque Area

1 Weems Gallery Old Town
The huge selection features crafts and jewelry, as well as folk, devotional, and fine art. Also represents 200 local artists. ◈ Map N5 • 303 Romero St • 505-764-0302 • www.weemsgallery.com

2 Bien Mur Indian Market Center
Superb range of handmade Native American Southwestern arts and crafts, owned and operated by Sandia Pueblo. ◈ Map C6 • Tramway Rd, I-25 exit 234 • 505-821-5400

3 Patrician Design
An eclectic gathering of fine, decorative, and functional art by New Mexican artists. Linked with an interior-design studio, the gallery exhibits original paintings, sculpture, pottery, furniture, clothing, and jewelry. ◈ Map C6 • 216 Gold Ave SW • 505-242-7646

4 DSG Fine Art
Elegant gallery, representing New Mexico's finest contemporary artists such as Arturo Chavez and Frank McCulloch. ◈ Map C6 • 510 14th St SW • 505-266-7751

5 Mariposa Gallery
An award-winning Nob Hill gallery, offering New Mexico folk art and contemporary crafts. One-of-a-kind items in all price ranges are available. ◈ Map C6 • 3500 Central Ave SE • 505-268-6828 • www.mariposa-gallery.com

6 Hispaniae
A visual feast of Hispanic culture and color. The fabulous range includes Mexican folk art, pottery, textiles, books, and cookware. ◈ Map N5 • 410 Romero St • 505-244-1533 • www.hispaniae.com

7 Cowboys & Indians Antiques
Museum-quality Native American, Western, and Hispanic art and artifacts, including Plains Indian beadwork, Navajo textiles, cowboy gear, and Western antiques. ◈ Map C6 • 4000 Central Ave SE • 505-255-4054 • www.cowboysandindiansnm.com

8 Natural History and Science Museum Store
Intriguing books, posters, movies, and educational toys for children and adults. Dinosaurs are a prominent feature here. ◈ Map P5 • 1801 Mountain Rd NW • 505-841-2800

9 Ooh! Aah! Jewelry
Feminine and fun, this unique jewelry store offers seasonally themed, affordable creations from around the world. Semi-precious gems and baubles are part of the ever-changing offerings on display. ◈ Map C6 • 110 Amherst SE • 505-265-7170

10 Downtown Contemporary Art Center
Located in a historic building, this exciting contemporary art gallery showcases established as well as up-and-coming artists. ◈ Map C6 • 105 Fourth St SW • 505-242-1983

100

Galleries and shops are usually open daily, though some may be closed on Mondays, weekends, or holidays. Call for timings.

Price Categories

For a three-course meal for one, with half a bottle of wine (or equivalent meal), including taxes and extra charges.	$ under $20
	$$ $20–40
	$$$ $40–55
	$$$$ $55–80
	$$$$$ over $80

Above **Artichoke Café**

TOP 10 Places to Eat

1 Artichoke Café
One of Albuquerque's finest dining rooms offers a sophisticated menu. ◈ Map C6 • 424 Central Ave SE • 505-243-0200 • Dis. access • $$$

2 Church Street Café
Many of the New Mexican entrées at this historic restaurant are recipes that have been in the Ruiz family for four generations. ◈ Map P5 • 2111 Church St NW • 505-247-8522 • $$

3 El Patio
At this very popular New Mexican spot, classic enchiladas, burritos, and tacos can be ordered vegetarian-style or with meat. Tasty *sopaipillas*. ◈ Map C6 • 142 Harvard St SE • 505-268-4245 • Dis. access • $

4 Thai Crystal
Elegant dining room, serving authentic Thai cuisine. Attractions include a large selection of spicy curries. ◈ Map C6 • 109 Gold Ave SW • 505-244-3344 • $$

5 Graze!
Popular with Nob Hill locals, the eclectic seasonal menu always includes steak and seafood. ◈ Map C6 • 3128 Central Ave SE • 505-268-4729 • $$$

6 Gold Street Café
This legendary breakfast and lunch spot serves gourmet coffees and espresso. ◈ Map C6 • 218 Gold Ave SW • 505-765-1633 • Open for dinner Tue–Sat • $$

7 Scalo Northern Italian Grill
The exceptional seasonally changing menu at this chic, Art Deco gem features classic Northern Italian cuisine. ◈ Map C6 • 3500 Central Ave SE • 505-255-8781 • $$$

8 Sadie's
This New Mexican restaurant serves classics such as *carne adovada*, spicy beef burritos, and chicken enchiladas. ◈ Map C6 • 6230 4th St NW • 505-345-5339 • $$

9 Yanni's Mediterranean Bar & Grill
Moussaka, steaks, grilled seafood, and other Mediterranean favorites are served. The vegetarian menu is exceptional. ◈ Map C6 • 3109 Central Ave NE • 505-268-9250 • $$

10 Quarters BBQ
Barbeque spare ribs, chicken, brisket, and sausage with a tangy sauce have made this a popular choice for over 30 years. Some vegetarian entrées. ◈ Map C6 • 801 Yale Blvd SE • 505-843-7505 • $$

Locally popular El Patio restaurant

Unless otherwise stated, all restaurants are open daily, accept credit cards, and serve vegetarian dishes.

STREETSMART

SANTA FE, TAOS, & ALBUQUERQUE'S TOP 10

Left **Tourist reading a local daily** Center **Traveling with children and pets** Right **Santa Fe Opera**

⓾ Planning Your Trip

1 Visitors' Centers
For any tourist information, check with the New Mexico Visitors' Center in Santa Fe, or look up the *Santa Fe Visitor's Guide, Albuquerque Visitor's Guide,* and *Taos Vacation Guide.* The Indian Pueblo Cultural Center *(see p98)* offers input on Native American attractions.

2 Media
The *Albuquerque Journal* is the major state-wide newspaper, while the *Santa Fe New Mexican* offers a more political slant. The best sources for entertainment news are the free weeklies, the *Santa Fe Reporter* and *Alibi.*

3 Arts Information on the Internet
A wealth of specialized information is available on the Internet for art buffs. Websites with helpful insights are www.collectorsguide.com and www.insidesf.com.

4 Maps
Basic road maps and local attraction maps are available at the visitors' centers. The PLIC (Public Lands Information Center) offers maps of recreation areas. The *Automobile Club* maps give a good overview, while *The Horton Family Map* is an excellent local street atlas. *Travel Bug* carries USGS topo maps for serious hikers.

5 Visas and Identification
For visa information, all international travelers should check with their embassy or the US Department of State website (www.state.gov), well ahead of arrival date.

6 Insurance
Obtain travel and medical insurance before arriving in the US. When renting a car, make certain that adequate insurance coverage for accident and theft is included.

7 When to Visit
Santa Fe is, by and large, a year-round destination with 300 days of sunshine. Despite rain and cold spells, April to early June is the best time for whitewater rafting. July and August are the peak tourist season, with the Santa Fe Opera and many festivals and events. September and October are pleasant and less crowded. November to March is ski season, and the Christmas holidays are another peak tourist time.

8 What to Take
Casual dress is the rule here, although more formal wear can be worn for the opera and gourmet dining. Avoid skimpy attire when visiting the Native pueblos *(see p112).* Dress suitably for the hot summer, and carry a light jacket for cool evenings. Spring and fall can be both hot and cold, and winter coats may be required on some spring days. Winter is cold and snowy, especially in the ski areas near Santa Fe and Taos.

9 How Long to Stay
A minimal exploration of Santa Fe's galleries, history, museums, and shops would take four days. Each of the scenic road trips may take a day, and then another day or two to explore Taos or Albuquerque would be ideal.

10 Traveling with Children
Albuquerque is a famous children's destination *(see p56–7),* with many attractions around the Old Town that are fun for children. Bandelier National Monument is popular, and there are numerous outdoor activities in the area. The museums and attractions of Santa Fe and Taos are largely adult oriented.

Directory

Visitors' Centers
• *Albuquerque Convention Visitors Bureau:* 800-284-2282
• *New Mexico Department of Tourism:* 800-545-2070
• *PLIC:* 505-438-7542
• *Taos Visitor Center:* 800-348-0696

Preceding pages: **Walkway, The Shed restaurant**

Left **A scenic road to Taos** Right **A road sign**

🔟 Getting There

1 Albuquerque International Sunport (ABQ)

Sunport is the major airport for travel to Albuquerque, Santa Fe, and Taos. There are no direct international flights, but international carriers including American Airlines, Delta Airlines, and United Airlines fly into Sunport. Southwest Airlines offers the largest number of flights at Sunport.

2 Airport Shuttles, Buses, and Taxis

Taxis into Albuquerque are available from fixed points at the terminal. Sun Tran buses run every 30 minutes, stopping at signs marked with a sunburst. Shuttle service is available from the airport into Albuquerque, Santa Fe, and Taos.

3 Santa Fe Municipal Airport (SAF)

A limited number of commercial flights are available to Denver, Colorado, on Great Lakes Aviation. Private and charter flights predominate at this local airport. Roadrunner Shuttle runs a shuttle service to downtown Santa Fe.

4 Taos Municipal Airport (TSM)

The airport is mainly used for private and charter flights. Shuttle service to Taos can be found from Faust's

Transportation, and Enterprise car rental is located at the airport.

5 Amtrak Train

The Southwest Chief stops in Lamy, south of Santa Fe, on its route from Chicago to Los Angeles. The Lamy Shuttle provides service to Santa Fe with prior reservation. Albuquerque also has an Amtrak station, and offers service to many cities.

6 Greyhound Buses

Santa Fe, Taos, and Albuquerque have Greyhound bus terminals, which join into the nationwide Greyhound bus system.

7 By Car

Albuquerque lies at the junction of two major cross-country Interstates. I-25 from Denver passes through Santa Fe on the way south to Albuquerque, while I-40 connects Albuquerque with California and Oklahoma City. The city of Taos is located north of Santa Fe via NM 84.

8 Car Rental

Among the many national car rental firms, Avis and Hertz offer cars at various locations in Albuquerque. The selection is almost as large in Santa Fe, while Taos offers a few choices.

9 Car Travel

A car is the most practical and convenient

way to travel throughout the area, since many of the best sights and attractions are located outside of the small Old Town areas of each of the three cities *(see p106)*.

10 Emergency Services

In case of an emergency, dial 911. Each city has its own municipal police department, and each pueblo has its own tribal police department *(see p112)*. The New Mexico State Police or the county sheriff's department is available to provide assistance outside city limits *(see p110)*.

Directory

Airports
- Sunport: 505-244-7700
- SAF: 505-955-2901
- TSM: 575-758-4995

Airport Shuttles and Buses
- Enterprise: 505-474-3234
- Faust's Transportation: 505-758-3410
- Roadrunner Shuttle: 505-424-3367
- Sunport Shuttle: 505-883-4966
- ABQ Ride: 505-243-7433

Amtrak Train
- 505-842-9650
- www.amtrak.com

Greyhound Buses
- 800-231-2222

Car Rental
- Avis: 505-842-4080
- Hertz: 800-654-3131

Left **Parking outside St. Francis Church** Center **Road signs** Right **Strollers, Burro Alley**

Getting Around

By Car
Driving is the most popular and practical means of travel in this region. Parking is limited in the historic central areas of Santa Fe and Taos, but there are public parking lots near the Plaza and well-monitored parking meters along the streets (there is a hefty fine for an expired meter). Parking in Albuquerque is more plentiful and convenient. The cities have numerous gas stations, but in some outlying areas there may be as much as 60 miles (97 km) between stations.

Walking
The best way to explore central Taos, Albuquerque Old Town, and Santa Fe and Canyon Road is by walking. The streets are narrow and lined with fascinating shops, galleries, museums, and historic sights that make walking not only essential, but also a nice experience.

Santa Fe Buses
The city bus system, Santa Fe Trails, offering 9 major routes, links some of the outlying attractions with Santa Fe Plaza. The "M" bus to Museum Hill from the Plaza is the most useful route for travelers.

By Rail
Rail Runner Express, New Mexico's rail system, fully opened in December 2008. It runs from Belen to Sandoval County, connecting Sunport International Airport, Albuquerque and Santa Fe.

Santa Fe Taxis
There are limited taxis in Santa Fe, and there are no cab stands, Booking is essential. To arrange a ride, phone ahead to schedule a pick-up. All fares are metered.

Santa Fe Tipsy Tow Service
New Mexico has strict drunk-driving prohibitions, but on major holidays (only) you can call AAA for a pick-up if you are tipsy. The driver and the car but no passengers will be given a one-way ride, free for up to 15 miles (24 km). Foreign visitors and non-members of AAA will also be assisted.

Taos Buses
The town of Taos operates the Chile Line, which runs north and south along NM 68, between Taos Pueblo and the Rancho de Taos post office. In winter, Hertz (see p105) provides bus service to and from Taos Ski Valley. Call for dates and times of operation.

Taos Taxis
Taxi service is limited in Taos. However, it is available by calling Faust's Transportation (see p105) in advance. It is one of the airport shuttle operators in the area.

Albuquerque Buses
The city bus service provided by Sun Tran (see p105) offers good coverage, including downtown, Old Town, Nob Hill, and the airport. The bus stops are marked with a sunburst sign. Although the bus system is not as fast, convenient, or flexible as using a car, it is a practical way to visit these areas.

Albuquerque Taxis
Round-the-clock metered cab service is available throughout Albuquerque from two cab companies (see directory). However, you must call ahead to schedule a pick-up.

Directory

Santa Fe Buses
• "M" Buses: 505-955-2001

By Rail
• www.nmrailrunner.com

Santa Fe Taxis
• 505-438-0000

Santa Fe Tipsy Tow Service
• 800-AAA-HELP

Santa Fe Parking and Violations
• 505-955-6581

Taos Buses
• 575-751-4459

Albuquerque Taxis
• Albuquerque Cab Company: 505-883-4888
• Yellow-Checker Cab: 505-247-8888

Road quality in the cities and outlying areas is good. However, for exploring rural areas, a 4WD is recommended.

Left **People relaxing in a plaza** Center left **Sunhat** Center right **First-aid kit** Right **Water bottles**

🔟 Desert Precautions

1 Altitude
Santa Fe and Taos are both at 7,000 ft (2,134 m) above sea level, and Taos Ski Valley is even higher at 9,000 ft (2,743 m). If you are arriving from much lower altitudes, allow a few days to adapt to the altitude before engaging in strenuous activity. If visiting Albuquerque as well, plan the first days there as the altitude is lower and the climate more moderate, allowing adjustment to take place in stages.

2 Temperature Change
Temperatures can change rapidly in the desert, and often drop as much as 40 degrees F (4.4 degrees C) when the sun goes down. Dress in layers and carry a sweater, especially during outdoor activities.

3 Dehydration
The desert climate is very dry, and using a skin moisturizer helps to alleviate the dry and itchy skin condition that is common here. Drink a lot of water, more than you would at a lower altitude. Hikers especially are advised to carry at least a gallon (4 liters) of water per day and per person with them.

4 Don't Travel Alone
It is advisable not to venture into the desert alone. Also, avoid hiking without a map and a good compass, even if you are equipped with a Global Positioning System (GPS).

5 Outdoor Cautions
The New Mexico wilderness is home to venomous creatures such as rattlesnakes, scorpions, and deadly spiders. Avoid their preferred habitats, located under rocks and in crevices. Outdoors, watch where you step, and do not turn over rocks or reach up to touch ledges.

6 Wildfire
In recent years, New Mexico has been under severe drought conditions, which heightens the risk of fire in wilderness areas. Use extreme caution with cigarettes and open-flame campfires. Wildfires travel rapidly, so if you spot smoke on the horizon, be prepared to leave the area quickly. Current wildfire information can be found on the Internet.

7 Sunscreen and Sunhat
The sun is intense in the dry desert climate. Make sure to apply sunscreen liberally when outdoors, and wear a wide-brimmed hat for added protection. Wear sunglasses to protect your eyes from the glare, especially when on the ski slopes.

8 Wildlife
Rattlesnakes may be encountered in the morning and evening when they seek warm locations. They generally do not strike unless threatened, so give them a wide berth. Scorpion stings can also be very serious, especially for children. Black widow and brown recluse spiders hide in shady places and can often be found outside buildings and in garages. If bitten or stung by any of these, seek medical help immediately. Other wild creatures, such as gila monsters, wild boar, and bears, generally avoid humans. It is unlikely that you will be attacked if you avoid their habitat.

9 Camping Cautions
Shake out clothes and shoes that have been on the ground for any length of time, and especially overnight, as scorpions or tarantulas may seek refuge in them. There are cougars and black bears in this area, so be certain to keep food out of tents, and stored where bears cannot reach them. Double check all campfires to make certain they are out before you leave the area.

10 First-Aid Kit
When traveling through the desert on foot or by car, carry a first-aid kit, as well as extra water, food, and warm clothing. Let someone know where you are going and when you plan to return.

For current information on wildfire, log on to the official website of the National Interagency Fire Center (www.nifc.gov).

Left **Cloud Cliff Bakery** Center **Millicent Rogers Museum** Right **Santa Fe Festival**

Budget Tips

1 Airline Deals

When flying into Albuquerque, always compare prices on various airlines before choosing a flight. Price comparison websites are useful in selecting the best flight for your schedule. Check prices on the individual airline websites before booking as they may have the lowest fare of all.

2 Hotel Discounts

The best rates are often obtained during the non-peak tourist seasons. Discounts may be offered to retirees, Auto Club members, military, and corporate employees. Find out from the hotel reservations specialist about special rates or packages, and compare the rate offered by the hotel's website.

3 Museum Passes

Santa Fe offers a four-day unlimited access pass to five museums. The Museum Association of Taos gives discounted year-round admission to Millicent Rogers Museum, Taos Art Museum at the Fechin House, E.L. Blumenschein Home and Museum, Harwood Museum of Art, and La Hacienda de los Martinez.

4 Package Deals

Call the Visitors' Centers and ask about hotel and local transportation packages that include tickets to major museums or events.

Also, look for airline packages online that include transportation or hotel accommodations at reduced rates.

5 Coupons

Before your hotel reservations are final, sign up for the free See New Mexico Discount Card which entitles you to discounts at hotels, restaurants, and tourist sights. Stop in at the Visitors' Center and ask for any coupons that are available.

6 Entertainment and Attractions

Some museums and attractions offer free or discounted entrance fees on certain days of the week. Seniors, students, children, and New Mexico residents can expect discounted rates.

7 Santa Fe Opera

The Santa Fe Opera *(see p74)* offers a variety of discounts, travel and ticket packages, and programs. These vary from year to year, but may include discounted family rehearsal nights, standing room-only tickets, and discounted opera tickets with airline travel packages.

8 Free Events

Numerous free festivals, special events, and summer concerts are held at the plazas, including Taos Plaza Live! and Albuquerque's

Summerfest. Santa Fe, Taos, and Albuquerque are also famous for art events presented by hundreds of fine galleries.

9 Restaurants

Lunch menus at popular restaurants are often far less expensive than dinner. Mexican restaurants, coffee-houses, cafés, and bakeries often serve hearty as well as light meals. Less expensive, they offer faster service than most of the other restaurants. Restaurants located away from popular tourist areas are sometimes cheap as well.

10 Travel Off-Season

Avoid the most popular tourist seasons, such as the summer months, festival and holiday weekends, Christmas season, and the late-winter ski season. If your schedule is flexible, call the hotels and ask when you can get the best rates. Airline fares, too, will be lowest.

Directory

Airline Deals
• www.expedia.com
• www.travelocity.com
• www.priceline.com

Coupons
• www.newmexico.org/seenm
• www.999dine.com

Cultural Events
• www.nmculturenet.org

Left **Disabled parking sign** Center **Curb outside Aztec Café** Right **A disabled-friendly venue**

TOP10 Special Needs Tips

1 What to Expect
Even though the historical areas are at least 300 years old, wheelchair access is decent in the three areas. Santa Fe is more sensitive to the needs of tourists with disabilities compared to Taos, where easy accessibility is confined mostly to its Plaza area.

2 Disabled Parking
Parking spots for the disabled are available, but they tend to fill quickly in the popular tourist areas. Many businesses allot special parking places near the front door. Santa Fe has spacious disabled parking spots near the State Capitol building.

3 Make Reservations and Ask
Call ahead for clarification, in case of any personal needs. Many shops and galleries in the old areas have steps leading to the doorway. A gallery or restaurant may provide an alternate entrance for a wheelchair, or help with parking on request.

4 Public Transportation
Santa Fe's public transportation system offers good wheelchair accessibility. The buses have lifts, and generally the stops are well-located. However, outside of the Plaza area, you may have to locate an appropriate drop-off point. The lifts in Taos and Albuquerque buses, however, are not as advanced as those in Santa Fe. The taxis either have wheelchair access, or can make alternate arrangements.

5 Hotels
The newest and largest hotels offer the best accessibility If you use a reservation service or travel agent to make your reservation, always call the hotel direct to discuss specific needs. Older hotels and smaller properties are often less accessible and offer fewer special services for hearing- and visually-impaired visitors.

6 Restaurants
Be sure to make a reservation in advance, especially during peak tourist seasons and dining hours. It is always best to ask detailed questions about accessibility.

7 Ramped Curbs
The historic Plaza areas offer very good wheelchair access for the most part. Although some of the crossing curbs and access ramps do not meet the latest standards, they are navigable.

8 Car Rental
Quite a few large auto rental firms offer rental vehicles that meet a broad variety of needs. Be sure to get confirmation that they will supply a vehicle with the exact features you require.

Wheelchair Getaways in Albuquerque offers vehicles for rent with lifts for wheelchair users.

9 The Governor's Commission on Disability
The friendly staff here can answer queries regarding your trip. The Access-Able Travel Source and the Society for Accessible Travel & Hospitality are national organizations offering advice on traveling for the disabled.

10 Ski Program
Since 1985, the Adaptive Ski Program has offered safe and supportive ski lessons suitable for a broad range of physical and developmental disabilities. Lessons for adults and children are offered at Sandia Peak *(see p98)* and Ski Santa Fe *(see p74)*.

Directory

Car Rental
• *Wheelchair Getaways: 505-247-2626*

The Governors Commission on Disability
• *Access-Able Travel Source: 303-232-2979*
• *Society for Accessible Travel and Hospitality: 212-447-7284*

Ski Program
• *Adaptive Ski Program: 505-995-9858*

Left **Logo of the Santa Fe police** Center **Mural outside a clinic** Right **Always carry your passport**

Security and Health

1 Keeping Documents Safe

Before leaving home, make photocopies of all important documents such as passport and visa, as well as the serial numbers of traveler's checks and credit cards. International visitors must contact their embassy in case of a lost passport, or an emergency.

2 Crime

New Mexicans are very friendly, but many of them are also very poor. Observing a few guidelines might minimize the risk of crime. Never carry large amounts of cash. Sling handbags and cameras over one shoulder with the strap across your body.

3 Hospitals

All three areas have very good hospitals. Call your insurance provider for a referral to a local clinic or doctor.

4 Walk-in Clinics

For minor injuries or non-emergency medical needs, walk-in clinics offer great service on a pre-paid basis if you do not have insurance, or for your standard co-pay if you have one.

5 Pharmacies

Pharmacies are located throughout Santa Fe, Taos, and Albuquerque. In case you need a pharmacy late at night, these also offer extended hours.

6 Emergency

Dial 911 for all emergencies, medical, police, or fire. There are hospitals with emergency rooms throughout Taos, Santa Fe, and Albuquerque. You can seek help from the police departments if you encounter any trouble.

7 Car Accident

Dial 911 if anyone is injured. Call the police if property damage appears to be over $500, or if you require a police report. Drivers must exchange driver's license information and all vehicle insurance details. If you are in a rental car, report accidents to the agency immediately.

8 Seatbelts

In New Mexico, the driver and all passengers in the car are legally bound to wear seatbelts. If not, expect to be pulled over by the police and ticketed. Children under the age of five and who weigh less than 40 lb (18 kg) must be secured in a car safety seat. If renting a car, request for a child safety seat in advance.

9 Public Restrooms

All major attractions, as well as gas stations and restaurants have public restrooms. Shopping centers, public buildings, libraries, and large hotels are other places to try.

10 Drunk Driving

New Mexico has one of the toughest drunk driving laws in the United States. Be certain to designate a non-drinking driver ahead of time, or arrange for a taxi to pick up your party and deliver you to your hotel *(see p105)*.

Directory

Hospitals
• Albuquerque: Prebysterian Hospital, 505-841-1234
• Santa Fe: St. Vincent Hospital, 505-983-3361
• Taos: Holy Cross Hospital, 575-758-8883

Walk-in Clinics
• Urgent Care Santa Fe, 505-474-0120
• OnCall Medical Services Santa Fe, 505-954-9949

Emergency
• Police Emergency: 911
• Police Non-Emergency: 505-242-2677 (Albuquerque); 505-428-3710 (Santa Fe); 575-758-2217 (Taos)

Pharmacies
• Walgreens: 505-255-5511 (Albuquerque); 505-982-4643 (Santa Fe)
• Taos Pharmacy: 575-758-3342 (Taos)

Hotlines
• Poison Control: 800-432-6866 • Rape Crisis Albuquerque: 505-266-7711 • Sexual Assault Santa Fe: 505-986-9111• Crisis Taos: 575-758-9888

Emergency care is offered by several local providers. Consult the yellow pages of the telephone book for details.

Left **Post boxes** Right **The First State Bank in Taos**

🔟 Banking and Communications

Exchange
Exchange some money before arrival. Banks provide the best exchange rates. However, in this area, only some of them will exchange money. For daily expenses, you can use credit cards, traveler's checks in US dollars, and ATM machines for cash withdrawals.

ATMs
There are 24-hour ATMs everywhere. Look on the back of the ATM or credit card to see which banking network it is associated with. ATMs inside convenience stores or malls charge for the convenience, as does your own bank if you go outside the network.

Banks
Most major banks can be found in the area. Banking hours are generally 9 or 10am to 5 or 6pm, Monday through Friday. Some banks are open Saturday mornings

Traveler's Checks
By far the safest form of money, traveler's checks in US dollars are accepted everywhere in Santa Fe, Taos, and Albuquerque. Change is given in cash. Lost or stolen traveler's checks are easily replaced.

Telephone
Before using a phone at a hotel, enquire about the specific charges for local and long-distance calls. Coin-operated pay phones can be found at hotels, and at some restaurants and gas stations, but very few of them take incoming calls.

Phone Cards
Pre-paid phone cards are readily available. Read the fine print before buying one. Be aware of the minimum calling charge, particularly for international calls.

Internet
Most hotel rooms are wired for Internet access, but check to see if the service is dial-up. Many of the larger hotels have business centers with Internet access. There are quite a few Internet cafés in central Santa Fe, and throughout Albuquerque and Taos as well. At most of these locations you will need a laptop equipped with a wireless card to use the Internet.

Post Offices
Normal post office hours are from 8:30am to 4:30pm Monday through Friday. Some branches are open on Saturday mornings. Stamps are either available from machines in the lobby, which have signs that indicate the cost of postage for domestic and international locations, or from the clerks behind the counter.

Courier Services
International and domestic packages can be shipped from either DHL or FedEx offices located in the major cities. Packages can also be sent through the post office or a UPS franchise.

Packing Services
A UPS franchise is ideal if you need boxes, packing materials, and tape to prepare your items for shipping. The UPS location will be able to ship the package domestically as well as internationally.

Left **Native Americans in festive gear** Right **Tourists observing a kiva from a distance**

🔟 Etiquette on Pueblo Lands

1 Sovereign Nations
The villages (pueblos) of the Pueblo people operate as sovereign entities within the US. They have their own well-trained police and fire departments as well as medical facilities.

2 Individual Laws
Each pueblo is a separate tribal group with its own laws and policies. Most pueblos that are open to the public post their rules in obvious places. It is recommended to read and follow them.

3 Privacy
The Pueblo tribes have kept their traditional life and ceremonies virtually unchanged since before European contact. This is partially because they have never been displaced by war, and partially because they have kept their religious and sacred ceremonies very private. The only rituals that outsiders can witness are the public ones such as the corn dance. Only some villages allow tourists, and all close frequently without advance notice.

4 Courtesy
Public ceremonies are still religious in nature, so visitors should behave as if they are in a church. Do not ask questions of the Native Americans during the ceremony and if you must speak, do so quietly.

5 Photography
Photography is a particularly sensitive issue with Pueblo Indians. Do not photograph an individual without their permission. Individuals may request a fee or tip (usually $2–$10) for allowing you to take their picture. Pueblos that are open to the public will often charge a "camera fee" that allows you to photograph buildings and objects in areas that are open to the public. Do not photograph inside churches. Avoid taking pictures of public ceremonies, unless you have express permission to do so. The same rules apply to audio recordings and sketches. When in doubt, ask for help.

6 Respect Private Homes
Most of the buildings in a pueblo are private homes. Entering a private home without permission is regarded as intrusive behavior. Do not enter any building that is not clearly marked as a shop or open to the public. Never enter a kiva, graveyard, or other sacred space.

7 Things to Avoid
It is a criminal offense to bring alcohol, drugs, or firearms into a pueblo. You may have to encounter the Pueblo police if you attempt to do so. Pay particular attention to, and obey, all posted speed limits.

8 Show Respect
When visiting a village, do not climb ladders or the walls, as some of the soft adobe walls can be several 100 years old and could crumble. Do not pick up, touch, or remove any artifacts or objects. Also, do not bring pets into a pueblo. If you have children with you, they need be kept close to you and under control at all times.

9 Be Reserved
As do most Native Americans tribes, the Pueblo Indians often find tourists' behavior to be loud and aggressive. When speaking to Natives, take care to speak quietly. Avoid eye contact and do not point at them, yourself, or at anything else, as it is considered rude. Avoid speaking excessively about yourself, or bragging. Do not offer to shake hands with Native Americans unless they gesture first, and then remember to do so gently.

10 Native Time
Time is a relative concept within the pueblos. A ceremony or event scheduled for 2pm may actually begin at 2:30 or 3pm. Be patient and wait. Always bear in mind that this is their unique culture and you are being allowed to experience it as a guest.

Left **Balloon View RV Park** Right **American RV Park**

🔟 RV Parks and Campgrounds

1 Santa Fe Skies RV Park

Open all year, this campground sits atop a plateau, offering mountain and desert views. Besides other attractions, the area also has a walking trail. Big rig sites, pull-thrus, and full hook-ups are available.

2 Rancheros de Santa Fe Campground

Just minutes from central Santa Fe, this large park with hiking trails is open mid-March to October. Most sites are wooded, and big rig sites, pull-thrus, full hook-ups, and cabins can be found.

3 Santa Fe KOA Campground

Set in the foothills of the Sangre de Cristo Mountains, this campground features large, shady sites, laundry facilities, a camp store, and a personal escort to your site. It is open March to October, and provides pull-thrus, full hook-ups, and tent sites.

4 Los Campos de Santa Fe RV Resort

An in-town location close to Santa Fe Plaza, with its city bus service, makes this campground a practical alternative. Shopping of all types is located nearby on busy Cerrillos Road. Pull-thrus and full hook-ups are available. Open all year.

5 Sierra Village Vacation Park

Located on the Enchanted Circle *(see p94)*, this small campground has just a few big rig capable sites, and is best suited for small RVs or tents. Full hook-ups and tent sites. Open June–September.

6 Taos Valley RV Park & Campground

Situated in high-desert country with mountain views, this campground is located 3 miles (5 km) south of Taos Plaza. Big rig sites, pull-thrus, full hook ups, and tent sites. Open all year.

7 Orilla Verde Recreation Area

South of Rancho de Taos, this recreation area is a favorite location for hikers and campers. Three of the four campgrounds offer very few amenities. Partial hook-ups and tent sites. Open seasonally.

8 Albuquerque Central KOA

Conveniently located near the major thoroughfares, with views of the Sandia Mountains, a swimming pool, and RV rentals. Big rig sites, pull-thrus, full hook-ups, tent sites, and cabins. Open all year.

9 American RV Park

This beautiful, landscaped park provides executive sites with many modern amenities. Big rig sites, pull-thrus, and full hook-ups. Open all year.

10 Balloon View RV Park

Beautiful views with good access to Sandia Peak Aerial Tramway and Balloon Fiesta Park. Weekly and monthly rates offered. Pull-thrus and full hook-ups. Open all year.

Directory

Santa Fe Skies RV Park
• *14 Browncastle Ranch: 505-473-5946*

Rancheros de Santa Fe Campground
• *Old L. Vegas Hwy I-25; 505-466-3482*
• *www.rancheros.com*

Santa Fe KOA Campground
• *934 Old L.Vegas Hwy I-25; 505-466-1419*

Los Campos de Santa Fe RV Resort
• *3574 Cerrillos Rd; 505-473-1949*

Sierra Village Vacation Park
• *US Hwy 64, Taos; 575-758-3660*

Taos Valley RV Park & Campground
• *120 Este Es Rd; 575-758-4469*

Albuquerque Central KOA
• *12400 Skyline Rd NE; 505-296-2729*

American RV Park
• *I-40 Westside Exit 149; 505-831-3545*

Balloon View RV Park
• *500 Tyler Rd NE Albuquerque; 505-345-3716*

Left **La Fonda, Santa Fe** Right **La Posada de Santa Fe Resort & Spa**

TOP 10 Luxury Hotels: Santa Fe

1 La Posada de Santa Fe Resort & Spa
Close to the Plaza, this luxury resort features original art from the best local galleries in many of the elegantly appointed guest rooms and the common areas. ✪ *Map L4 • 330 E Palace Ave • 505-986-0000 • Dis. access • www.laposadadesantafe. com • $$$$$*

2 Bishop's Lodge Resort & Spa
One of the Southwest's most renowned luxury retreats, this unique ranch setting offers recreation, easy access to the nearby Santa Fe Ski Area, as well as plush rooms, fine dining, and a superb spa. ✪ *Map M1 • Bishop's Lodge Rd • 505-983-6377 • Dis. access • www. bishopslodge.com • $$$$$*

3 Hacienda del Cerezo
The exclusive resort offers an all-inclusive package including gourmet meals and horseback riding across private ranchland. Plush suites have private patios with scenic views. ✪ *Map D4 • 100 Camino del Cerezo • 505-982-8000 • www.haciendadelcerezo. com • $$$$$*

4 Hyatt Regency Tamaya Resort & Spa
Situated along the banks of the Rio Grande River, this luxury destination-style resort features elegant guest rooms with private balconies and ultra-modern amenities. The architecture is reminiscent of a Native American pueblo, with charming artwork and vast courtyards. Activities include a golf course, fitness center, and riding stables. ✪ *Map C5 • 1300 Tuyuna Trail, Santa Ana Pueblo • 505-867-1234 • Dis. access • www. tamaya.hyatt.com • $$$$$*

5 Vista Clara Ranch Spa Resort
This recently-renovated resort offers adobe guest rooms and *casitas* with patios, fireplaces, and soaking tubs. Resort facilities include an art studio, equestrian center, ozone pool, workshops, and hiking trails. ✪ *Map D5 • Galisteo • 505-466-4772 • Partial dis. access • www. vistaclara.com • $$$$$*

6 Eldorado Hotel
Just blocks from Santa Fe Plaza, this hotel draws business and experienced travelers, thanks to its high level of personalized attention, fine dining, and nightly entertainment. ✪ *Map H3 • 309 W. San Francisco St • 505-988-4455 • Dis. access • www. eldoradohotel.com • $$$$$*

7 Hotel Santa Fe
Recently declared one of the top 500 hotels in the world, this pueblo-style boutique hotel is the city's only Native American-owned hotel. Its highlights are the stunning Native and Southwestern decor, Pueblo art, and programs including traditional dances and flute music in summer. ✪ *Map H6 • 1501 Paseo de Peralta • 505-982-1200 • Dis. access • www. hotelsantafe.com • $$$$*

8 La Fonda
The captivating lobby of this historical hotel boasts renowned art works on the walls with hand-painted details. Blending the modern and traditional, the rooms offer handcrafted decor and high-speed Internet (see p64). ✪ *Map K4 • 100 E San Francisco St • 505-982-5511 • Dis. access • www.lafondasantafe.com • $$$$$*

9 Hotel Plaza Real
This boutique-style hotel offers suites and rooms with handcrafted furniture, fireplaces, and the Internet. ✪ *Map K3 • 125 Washington Ave • 505-988-4900 • Partial dis. access • $$$$*

10 Hotel St. Francis
This 1880 National Trust hotel presents old-world elegance. Rooms have high ceilings, brass or iron beds, and cherry and oak furnishings. ✪ *Map J4 • 210 Don Gaspar Ave • 505-983-5700 • Dis. access • www.hotelstfrancis.com • $$$$*

Unless otherwise stated, all hotels and inns accept credit cards, have private bathrooms and air conditioning.

Price Categories

For a standard,	
double room per	**$** under $70
night (with breakfast	**$$** $70–100
if included), taxes	**$$$** $100–150
and extra charges.	**$$$$** $150–200
	$$$$$ over $200

🔟 Luxury Inns: Santa Fe

1 Inn of the Five Graces

Luxury and convenience blend together in this historic inn, where the Wild West decor meets Oriental elegance. Luxurious rooms are tastefully decorated with rich tapestries, and soft featherbeds. ✎ *Map J5 • 150 E De Vargas St • 505-992-0957 • Dis. access • www. fivegraces.com • $$$$$*

2 Inn of the Anasazi

This inn mixes Southwest adobe style with Native American decor. The doors and sculptured stairways set the stage for fireside chats with local artists. Guest rooms offer four-poster beds and Native American art. ✎ *Map K3 • 113 Washington Ave • 505-988-3030 • Dis. access • www. rosewoodhotels.com • $$$$$*

3 Inn on the Alameda

Adobe walls and charming courtyards provide seclusion in this lovely inn. Richly appointed rooms have Southwestern decor. ✎ *Map L5 • 303 E Alameda • 505-984-2121 • Dis. access • www.inn-alameda.com • $$$$*

4 Inn at Loretto

This dramatic pueblo-style adobe inn is situated close to the Plaza and Canyon Road galleries. Lavish rooms come with carved furnishings and Native art on the walls. ✎ *Map K4 • 211 Old Santa Fe Trail • 505-988-5531 • Dis. access • www.innatloretto. com • $$$$$*

5 Houses of the Moon at Ten Thousand Waves

The Japanese-style inn is nestled in juniper and pine woods. Individual cottages are decorated with fine woodwork, and many of the rooms have fireplaces or private patios *(see p52)*. ✎ *Map M1 • 3451 Hyde Park Rd • 505-982-9304 • Partial dis. access • www. tenthousandwaves.com • $$$$*

6 Sunrise Springs Inn & Retreat

A Southwestern-style retreat, where guests enjoy sweat lodges, Japanese tea ceremonies, and tai chi *(see p53)*. ✎ *Map D5 • 242 Los Pinos Rd • 505-471-3600 • Partial dis. access • www. sunrisesprings.com • $$$*

7 Inn of the Governors

This tasteful adobe country inn is close to the Plaza and downtown museums. Breakfast buffet and afternoon tea included, as well as free parking. ✎ *Map J4 • 101 West Alameda • 505-982-4333 • Partial dis. access • www. innofthegovernors.com • $$$$*

8 El Farolito

Lovely *casitas*, with private baths and small patios, offer cozy B&B atmosphere in a small inn setting. Rooms are individually decorated to reflect Pueblo Indian, Spanish Colonial, or Pioneer Anglo heritages with original art and hand-crafted furniture. Most offer tile or brick floors, wood beamed ceilings, kiva fireplaces, and private entrances. ✎ *Map H5 • 514 Galisteo St • www.farolito.com • 505-988-1631 • $$$$$*

9 Hacienda Nicholas

This attractive adobe hacienda has classic Western decor. It also accepts pets. A breakfast buffet is included and spa treatments are available at the adjacent Victorian-style B&B Madeline Inn. ✎ *Map K3 • 320 E Marcy St • 505-986-1431 • www.haciendanicholas. com • $$$$*

10 Water Street Inn

Large, comfortable rooms are decorated with a charming blend of Native American, New Mexican, and cowboy art and artifacts. Each room is appointed in a different style, and most rooms have a fireplace. ✎ *Map G3 • 427 W Water St • 505-984-1193 • Partial dis. access • www. waterstreetinn.com • $$$$*

Left **Don Gaspar Inn** Right **Old Santa Fe Inn**

TOP 10 Mid-Range Hotels: Santa Fe

1 Inn of the Turquoise Bear

Housed in the historic home of poet and essayist Witter Bynner, this B&B-style inn has flower-filled gardens, old stone benches, and flagstone paths. Rooms have simple furnishings; most of them come with private baths. ✪ Map D4 • 342 E Buena Vista • 505-983-0798 • Partial dis. access • www. turquoisebear.com • $$$

2 Pueblo Bonito B&B Inn

Rooms at this lovely turn-of-the-20th century adobe have local art and some offer small kitchens. Once a private estate, the grounds feature courtyards, narrow brick paths, and majestic old shade trees. Breakfast and afternoon tea are included. ✪ Map H6 • 138 West Manhattan Ave • 505-984-8001 • www. pueblobonitoinn.com • $$$

3 Residence Inn by Marriott

Tasteful ambience and nightly social hours are offered at this inn. Quality bedding, suites with kitchens, and free high-speed Internet service are standard here. There are fireplaces in all the rooms. ✪ Map H5 • 1698 Galisteo St • 505-988-7300 • www. residenceinn.com • $$$$

4 Territorial Inn

This adults-only inn, near the Palace of the Governors, offers a variety of rooms, from large to quaint and cozy. ✪ Map K3 • 215 Washington Ave • 505-989-7737 • www. territorialinn.com • $$$$

5 Dancing Ground of the Sun

At this inn, located close to the historic Plaza and Canyon Road, all rooms and casitas are decorated with Southwestern-style furniture, complemented with Native American decor. Most of the rooms are spacious and have kitchens. ✪ Map L4 • 711 Paseo de Peralta • 505-986-9797 • www. dancingground.com • $$$$

6 Fort Marcy Hotel Suites

Spacious modern condominiums come with one-, two-, or three-bedroom units with full kitchens, living-rooms, and fireplaces. The conveniently located hotel offers a heated pool and many rooms have spectacular views. ✪ Map L2 • 300 Kearny • 505-988-2800 • www. fortmarcy.com • $$$$

7 Don Gaspar Inn

This intimate inn offers beautifully landscaped grounds. Three historic houses come with three distinct architectural styles – Territorial, Pueblo Revival, and Arts and Crafts. The rooms are spacious, sunny, and tastefully decorated. ✪ Map J6 • 623 Don Gaspar Ave • 505-986-8664 • Partial dis. access • www. dongaspar.com • $$$$

8 El Rey Inn

This 1930s-style motel has been remodeled with lovely garden areas and individually furnished rooms that include antiques and upholstered chairs and sofas. Some rooms have kitchenettes. ✪ Map L2 • 1862 Cerrillos Inn • 505-982-1931 • Partial dis. access • www.elreyinnsantafe. com • $$$

9 Lodge at Santa Fe

Comfortable and family-friendly, this two-story hotel offers good value. Two-bedroom condos, on-site parking, exercise room, and heated outdoor pool. ✪ Map L2 • 750 N St. Francis Dr • 505-992-5800 • www.lodgeatsantafe. com • $$$$

10 Old Santa Fe Inn

Close to the Plaza, this family-oriented inn provides an attractive and inviting common area with fireplace. Guest rooms are furnished with New Mexican-style furniture and textiles. Complimentary breakfast is served in the dining room. ✪ Map H5 • 320 Galisteo St • 505-995-0800 • Dis. access • www. oldsantafeinn.com • $$$$

Unless otherwise stated all hotels accept credit cards, have private bathrooms and air conditioning.

Price Categories

For a standard, double room per night (with breakfast if included), taxes and extra charges.

$	under $70
$$	$70–100
$$$	$100–150
$$$$	$150–200
$$$$$	over $200

Above **Garrett's Desert Inn**

TOP10 Budget Hotels: Santa Fe

1 Garrett's Desert Inn

This family-run 1956 motor-inn style lodging has on-site parking, a restaurant, and heated swimming pool. Rooms are available for a range of prices. ⊗ Map K4 • 311 Old Santa Fe Trail • 505-982-1851• www.garrottsdesertinn.com • $$$

2 Courtyard by Marriott, Santa Fe

Good value for money, this hotel has rooms with refrigerators, high-speed Internet, and dual phone lines. Other facilities at this well-equipped establishment include two spas, an indoor swimming pool, an exercise room, and on-site parking. ⊗ Map L2 • 3347 Cerrillos Rd • 505-473-2800 • Dis. access • $$

3 Silver Saddle Motel

This adobe motel has appealing Southwestern decor. It was remodeled quite a while ago, but the rooms are comfortable, clean, and extremely affordable. One of the best in its class along this stretch of Cerrillos Road. ⊗ Map L2 • 2810 Cerrillos Rd • 505-471-7663 • $

4 La Quinta Inn Santa Fe

This popular chain motel offers spacious, cozy rooms in a three-story building, with on-site parking, an outdoor swimming pool, and high-speed Internet access in every room. Tariff includes Continental breakfast. ⊗ Map L2 • 4298 Cerrillos Rd • 505-471-1142 • Dis. access • www.lq.com • $$

5 Sage Inn

This attractive modern adobe two-story motel provides affordable lodging, on-site parking, and a small heated outdoor swimming pool. All rooms are equipped with computer dataports. ⊗ Map L2 • 725 Cerrillos Rd • 505-982-5952 • www.santafesageinn.com • $$

6 Pecos Trail Inn

Set in the piñon pine wooded foothills of the Sangre de Cristo Mountains, this charming country inn is just a five-minute drive from the Plaza. Southwestern-style rooms are spacious; some come with kitchenettes. ⊗ Map L2 • 2239 Old Pecos Trail • 505-982-1943 • Dis. access • $$

7 Fairfield Inn Marriott

This modestly upscale chain hotel offers above-average comfort at an affordable price. Located north of I-25 on Cerrillos Road, it offers rooms with high-speed Internet, dual phone lines, free Continental breakfast, and a heated indoor pool. ⊗ Map L2 • 4150 Cerrillos Rd • 505-474-4442 • Dis. access • $$

8 Park Inn & Suites

This pleasantly appointed chain hotel has an attractive, spacious lobby. The accommodations are comfortable and the inn has wireless connections throughout. Some of the guest rooms have kitchenettes, and there is an outdoor swimming pool. ⊗ Map L2 • 2907, Cerrillos Rd • 505-471-3000 • www.parkinn.com/santafenm • $$

9 Inn on the Paseo

This small friendly inn combines Southwestern comfort with country charm in a convenient location within walking distance of the Plaza. Well-appointed guest rooms all have down comforters and patchwork quilts. ⊗ Map L3 • 630 Paseo de Peralta • 505-984-8200 • www.innonthepaseo.com • $$$

10 Santa Fe Motel & Inn

A charming inn within walking distance of the Plaza, which offers great value with all the right touches. The guest rooms are cheerful and cozy, the complimentary breakfast is satisfying, and the courtyard pleasant. There is high-speed Internet and on-site parking. Some of the rooms come with kitchenettes. ⊗ Map G5 • 510 Cerrillos Rd • 505-982-1039 • www.santafemotel.com • $$

Hotel rates vary widely according to day and season. Peak and most expensive times are weekends, summer, and winter holidays.

Left **American Artists Gallery House Bed & Breakfast** Right **The Historic Taos Inn**

🔟 Taos Hotels

1 The Historic Taos Inn

One of America's best-value inns is located close to the Plaza and attractions. The two-story lobby, open spaces, and Southwestern decor create an intimate atmosphere. Most rooms have fireplaces. ✎ *Map P2 • 125 Paseo del Pueblo Norte • 575-758-2233 • www.taosinn.com • $$$*

2 El Pueblo Lodge

Located on a four acre site slightly north of Taos, the lodge has spacious rooms, facilities for groups and a swimming pool. All rooms have baths and refrigerators. A light breakfast is included. ✎ *Map P2 • 412 Paseo del Pueblo Norte • 575-758-8700 • www.elpueblolodge.com • $$*

3 El Monte Sagrado

This stunning resort and spa combines the ultimate in luxury with natural beauty. Rooms are decorated with Native, international, and artistic themes. Two fine restaurants and world-class spa. ✎ *Map Q3 • 317 Kit Carson Rd • 575-758-3502 • Dis. access • www.elmontesagrado.com • $$$$$*

4 Casa de las Chimeneas

An oasis of calm, this plush B&B-style inn has a lovely courtyard garden. Cozy rooms with private entrances and fine linens. Breakfast, buffet supper served. A fitness room and outdoor hot tub are provided. ✎ *Map E2 • 405 Cordoba Rd • 575-758-4777 • www.visittaos.com • $$$$$*

5 American Artists Gallery House Bed & Breakfast

Decorated in Native American, Southwest, and Spanish themes, all rooms come with a private entrance and a fireplace. Complimentary breakfast served. ✎ *Map E2 • 132 Frontier Lane • 575-758-4446 • www.taosbedandbreakfast.com • $$$*

6 Don Fernando de Taos

Pueblo-style adobe hotel, with landscaped grounds, courtyards, and an atrium-style enclosed pool and hot tub. ✎ *Map P3 • 1005 Paseo del Pueblo Sur • 575-758-4444 • www.donfernandodetaos.com • $$$*

7 Sagebrush Inn

Housed in a 1920s adobe with hand-hewn *vigas*, kiva fireplaces, and courtyards, the inn is decorated with original Southwestern art, including Native rugs. A full breakfast is served. An outdoor swimming pool and indoor hot tubs are provided. ✎ *Map P3 • 1508 Paseo del Pueblo Sur • 575-758-2254 • www.sagebrushinn.com • $$$*

8 Earthship Rentals

These one-, two-, and three-bedroom, fully sustainable houses are part of the Earthship community *(see p95)*. The solar-powered, earth-sheltered dwellings recycle most of their water. Most units feature full kitchens, some have fireplaces, greenhouses and gardens. ✎ *Map E2 • US 64, 2 miles W of Rio Grande Bridge • 575-751-0462 • www.earthship.org • $$$*

9 Snakedance Condominiums

Located in the center of Taos Ski Valley, near the lifts, these one-, two-, and three-bedroom condos offer full kitchens, gas fireplace, satellite television, and Internet access. There is an on-site convenience store, deli, fitness facility, and a guest lounge. ✎ *Map E2 • Taos Ski Valley • 575-776-2277 • www.snakedancecondos.com • $$$$$*

10 Hacienda Rancho de Chimayó

The rooms in this elegant country hacienda feature antique furniture, as well as handwoven Chimayó upholstery. All rooms have fireplaces and open into the courtyard. Continental breakfast is included in the tariff. ✎ *Map D3 • County Rd 98 • 575-351-2222• Dis. access • www.ranchodechimayo.com • $$*

Unless otherwise stated, all hotels accept credit cards, have private bathrooms and air conditioning.

Price Categories

For a standard	**$** under $70
double room	**$$** $70–100
(with breakfast	**$$$** $100–150
if included), taxes	**$$$$** $150–200
and extra charges.	**$$$$$** over $200

Above **Albuquerque Marriott Pyramid North**

🔟 Albuquerque Hotels

1 La Posada de Albuquerque
Listed on the National Register of Historic Places, this Spanish Colonial boutique-style hotel was built in 1939 by Conrad Hilton. A-list guests have included John F. Kennedy and Bill Gates. ◈ *Map C6 • 125 2nd St NW• 505-242-9090 • Dis. access • www. laposada-abq.com • $$$$*

2 Hyatt Regency Albuquerque
This large hotel has a two-story lobby with marble pillars and boutique shops. Rooms feature regional decor and wireless Internet access. There's a fitness center, pool, and a full business center. ◈ *Map C6 • 330 Tijeras Ave • 505-842-1234 • Dis. access • www.hyatt.com • $$$$*

3 Brittania & W. E. Mauger Estate B&B
Built in 1897, this well-restored Queen Anne estate has leaded glass windows and fine oak woodwork. Rooms have beds with down comforters. Breakfast buffet. ◈ *Map C6 • 701 Roma Ave NW • 505-242-8755 • www. maugerbb.com • $$$*

4 Los Poblanos Inn
Originally a ranch house designed by John Gaw Meem (see p39) in 1934, this historic inn is surrounded by gardens and fields. The individually-themed rooms with private entrances come with down comforters and pillows as well as a fireplace. ◈ *Map C6 • 4803 Rio Grande Blvd NW • 505-344-9297 • www.lospoblanos.com • $$$$*

5 Bottger Mansion of Old Town
Victorian-style decor with charming rooms and a lovely courtyard at this historic mansion. All rooms have antique furnishings and down comforters, while some have four-poster beds, claw-foot tubs or tin ceilings. ◈ *Map P5 • 110 San Felipe St • 505 243 3639 • www.bottger.com • $$$$*

6 Wyndham Albuquerque Hotel
Large luxury hotel located close to the airport offers excellent service mainly for business travelers and families. A business center, tennis courts, outdoor swimming pool, fitness room, and a restaurant. ◈ *Map C6 • 2910 Yale Blvd SE • 505-843-7000 • Dis. access • www.wyndham.com • $$$*

7 Courtyard by Marriott
Close to the airport, this good-value hotel offers efficient service for tourists and business travelers. Fitness services are also provided. ◈ *Map C6 • 1920 Yale Blvd SE • 505-843-6600 • Dis. access • www.marriott. com • $$$*

8 Hotel Albuquerque at Old Town
This full-service New Mexican Heritage Hotel has a grand lobby with Territorial-style windows, Navajo rugs, and hand-forged chandeliers. It also has a New Mexican chapel, outdoor pavilion, and courtyard. ◈ *Map N4 • 800 Rio Grande Blvd NW • 505-843-6300 • Dis. access • $$$*

9 Albuquerque Marriott Pyramid North
Marriott's flagship full-service hotel features Aztec pyramid-style design and a stunning 10-story atrium with a waterfall. Rooms provide beds with down comforters, executive desks, and high-speed Internet. ◈ *Map C6 • 5151 San Francisco Rd NE • 505-821-3333 • Dis. access • www.marriott.com • $$$*

10 Motel 6
This motel chain is noted for its clean, affordable rooms. It is located two miles from Fiesta Park and has an outdoor swimming pool, on-site parking and coin-operated laundry room. ◈ *Map C6 • 8510 Pan American Freeway NE • 505-821-1472 • Partial dis. access • www. motel6.com • $*

Hotel rates vary by day and season. Most expensive times are weekends (weekdays in Albuquerque), summer, winter holidays.

119

General Index

Acknowledgements

The Author
Nancy Mikula's passion has been to explore America and discover its little-known attractions. Her articles on travel and history have appeared in numerous publications in the USA and Canada. She has also co-authored Dorling Kindersley's Eyewitness Guides to Arizona and the Grand Canyon; and the Southwest.

Main Photographer
Tony Souter

Additional Photography
David Cannon, Demetrio Carrasco, Philip Dowell, Lynton Gardiner, Steve Gorton and Karl Shone, Dave King, David Mager, Gunter Marx, Andrew McKinney, Neil Mersh, David Murray and Jules Selmes, Lloyd Park, Nick Pope, Steve Shott, Clive Streeter, Carol Wiley, Francesca Yorke

Fact Checker
Lyn Kidder

At DK INDIA:
Managing Editor Aruna Ghose
Project Editors Alka Thakur, Shonali Yadav
Project Designer Shruti Singhi
Senior Cartographer Suresh Kumar
Cartographer Kunal Singh
Picture Researcher Taiyaba Khatoon
Picture Research Assistance Sumita Khatwani
Indexer & Proofreader Pooja Kumari
DTP Co-ordinator Shailesh Sharma
DTP Designer Vinod Harish

At DK LONDON:
Publisher Douglas Amrine
Publishing Manager Scarlett O'Hara
Design Manager Mabel Chan
Senior Cartographic Editor Casper Morris
Senior DTP Designer Jason Little
Senior Revisions Coordinator Claire Jones
Revisions Coordinators Rose Hudson, Pollyanna Poulter
Revisions Assistant Emma Anacootee
DK Picture Library Romaine Werblow, Myriam Meghrabi
Production Inderjit Bhullar

Picture Credits
t-top; tl-top left; tlc-top left center; tc-top center; tr-top right; cla-center left above; ca-center above; cra-center right above; cl-center left; c-center; cr-center right; clb-center left below; cb-center below; crb-center right below; bl-bottom left; b-bottom; bc-bottom center; bcl-bottom center left; br-bottom right; d-detail.

The works of art have been reproduced with permission of the following copyright holders: Bob Haozous: 43tr; GEORGIA O'KEEFFE MUSEUM: Georgia O'Keeffe: *Blue Flower*, 1918 Pastel on paper mounted to cardboard 20 x 16 in. Promised gift, The Burnett Foundation © 1987, Private Collection 6clb, 14-15c, *Ram's Head, Blue Morning Glory*, 1938 Oil on canvas, 20 x 30 in. Georgia O'Keeffe Museum Promised gift, The Burnett Foundation 15tl, *Black Iris VI*, 1936 Oil on canvas 36 x 24 in. Loan, Private Collection © Private Collection 15cra.

The publisher would like to thank the following individuals, companies and picture libraries for their kind permission to reproduce their photographs.

ALAMY: Ambient Images Inc./ Peter Bennett 18-19; Jon Arnold Images 3tl; Ernesto Burciaga 36tl; Bruce Coleman Inc. 32-33; Cosmo Condina 7cra; Robert Fried 96cr; Neil Setchfield 6tr; Stock Connection Distribution 3tr; Visions of America LLC 25 bl.

CORBIS: 14bc, 34tr; Bettmann 34bc, 35tr, 39tr; Tom Bean 36br; Richard Cummins 3br, 7br, 34tc, 97tr; Richard A. Cooke 25br; George H. H. Huey 30-31c; Dewitt Jones 82br; Wolfgang Kaehler 22-23c; Kelly-Mooney Photography 6crb; Lake County Museum 22cla; Charles & Josette Lenars 111tr; Marc Muench 86-87; Richard T. Nowitz 26-27c, 27tl.

EVO GALLERY: courtesy Herbert Lötz 19tl

GEORGIA O'KEEFFE MUSEUM: 14tr, 14cla, 15cb.

HARWOOD MUSEUM: 42bl.

INN & SPA AT LORETTO: 52tr, 52b. LA POSADA DE SANTA FE: 52tc.

MASTERFILE: Miles Ertman 4-5; J. A. Kraulis 96t; Curtis Strauss 1c.

MALCOM COULSON: 55br.

PAUL FRANKLIN: 3bl, 6cla, 7t, 7clb, 8-9c, 12-13c, 20tr, 42tr, 46bl, 55tl, 88cr, 90t, 102-103.

SHIDONI FOUNDRY INC.: 38br, 76tr.

THE BISHOP'S LODGE RANCH RESORT AND SPA: 53tr.

THE SANTA FE OPERA: Robert Reck 70-71, 74tr, 104tr.

TOPFOTO: 35tl.

FRONT FLAP: CORBIS: Jan Butchofsky-Houser cr; PAUL FRANKLIN: cl; LONELY PLANET PICTURE LIBRARY: tr.

All other images are © Dorling Kindersley. For further information see www.dkimages.com.

Acknowledgements

Special Editions of DK Travel Guides

DK Travel Guides can be purchased in bulk quantities at discounted prices for use in promotions or as premiums. We are also able to offer special editions and personalized jackets, corporate imprints, and excerpts from all of our books, tailored specifically to meet your own needs.

To find out more, please contact:

(in the US) **SpecialSales@dk.com**

(in the UK) **TravelSpecialSales@uk.dk.com**

(in Canada) DK Special Sales at **general@tourmaline.ca**

(in Australia) **business.development@pearson.com.au**

Street Index